MW00427241

From
Mother to Mother

ON THE LOSS OF A CHILD

From Mother to Mother © 2017 Emily R. Long.

All rights reserved. This book or any portion thereof
may not be reproduced or used in any manner whatsoever
without the express written permission of the publisher
except for the use of brief quotations in a book review.

Printed in the United States of America
First Printing 2017
978-0-9965556-7-8

Firefly Grace Publishing
Burlington, VT 05403
www.EmilyRLong.com

Interior and Cover Design: ShiftFWD
Author Photo: Greeta Soderholm

Gratitudes

For Amy Hermodson

Before I could speak of my losses aloud,
Before I could see out of the darkness of my pain,

You were there.
You sat with me,
You talked with me,
You offered chocolate.

I will never forget your kindness
or the simple gift of your presence in my darkest days.

Thank you.

Always,
For my Grace and Lily.

A special and profoundly grateful
THANK YOU
to all the mamas who shared their heart for this book.
You make this thing called life after loss infinitely brighter.

Other Available Books by Emily:

Invisible Mothers: When Love Doesn't Die (September 2015)

You Are Not Alone: Love Letters from Loss Mom to Loss Mom (April 2016)

From Father to Father: Letters from Loss Dad to Loss Dad (November 2016)

Life Without the Baby Journal: Redefining Life, Self, and Motherhood After Loss (April 2017)

Coming Soon:

Tending the Broken Hearted: How to Support Those Who Grieve

SWEET MAMA,

I wish I could be there with you now, in person, to hug you and hold you through these darkest of days after the loss of your precious child. I wish that I could sit with you, pour you a cup of comforting hot cocoa or tea, tuck a warm blanket around you and simply be with you while you learn to breath and be in this new world called life after loss.

In a way, that's what this book is, a way for myself and many other mothers who are living through what you are experiencing now to sit and be with you. We are here holding you close in our hearts as we can't do with our arms.

It is true that no words and no actions could ever fix what has happened – we cannot bring your precious child(ren) back for you, just as we could not prevent the loss of our own children. Even our fierce and absolute mama love could not save them and that is the unbearable sorrow that we all now live with every day.

I do believe, however, that the words that we share and the ways in which we who grieve reach out and touch each other help. No words or actions can fix our losses, but we can help pull each other through these dark hours of grief and pain. That is what I and every mother in this book are doing – reaching out to help all of us through our darkest hours.

This grief is not a burden that anyone should have to bear alone. We are here.

My hope is that this book is something that you can hold onto, in those dark, lonely and desperate moments of grief and pain and loss. This is a book you can open to any page and read the love-filled words of another mama like you who knows the pain of not being able to hold or see or hear the one you love most in the world. A reminder in the midst of grief and tears that you are not alone and you are loved. Because, Mama, you are so very loved.

These words and letters are written from our hearts to yours, from one mother to another. With open arms and big hearts, we welcome you (though we desperately wish we didn't have to) into our tribe of sisters – the community of mothers who know this unspeakable loss and grief. More importantly than the loss, however, we know the same beautiful, fierce mother love that lives in your heart – deep and abiding love for the child you cannot hold or see or hear yet who is alive in your heart each and every moment.

It is my hope that within these pages you will find love and moments of comfort. It is my hope that you will feel, deep down into your bones, that you are not alone and that you are so very loved. It is my hope that you will know without a doubt that your baby and your motherhood matter. It is my hope that you will know that your baby's life, however brief, has touched this world in irrevocable and valuable ways. It is my hope that this love and these words will help carry you through the darkest moments of your grief and show you glimmers of light in that darkness.

Not every letter will resonate with you. Not every experience shared here will speak to you. But there are many letters here and many different experiences – find the ones that speak to your heart and simply leave the ones that don't. All are offered with love and compassion and a desire to reach out to another mother who hurts so very much.

I cannot fix this loss and I cannot take away your pain, but will all my hopes and all my love, I offer you this book full of love and letters from our hearts to yours. And if you get nothing else from it, please know this:

You are not alone.
You love and you are loved.

And love never dies.

xoxo,
Emily

LETTERS

DEAR FELLOW LOSS MOMMY,

I know this isn't where you thought your life would be. Honestly, who does? Who is excited to enter this club? The child loss club. I wish I could be joyful and jumping up and down to welcome you. I do, however, have a welcoming hug. I am so sorry this is our lives now.

A mother's intuition is never wrong, and I knew from the time the pregnancy test was positive that something wasn't right. My 3rd child, Emma, was diagnosed with Trisomy 18 while in utero at 19 weeks. The form of trisomy she had made her incompatible with life. After all the testing was done I was given the option to abort her. I will never forget at that very moment she starting kicking me. She was here for a purpose. A purpose my husband & I would later come to understand. Emma lived for a beautiful 28 hours and 3 minutes. After that day, I changed. Or was the world around me changed?

It has been 18 months since we laid Emma to rest and in that time, this is what I know:

Cry! Don't be afraid to let it out. Even if it is every single day. Just cry.

The statement that says the truest of friends will stick around for the storm to clear is 100 % fact. I can count on one hand the people who still check on me daily. The sad truth is some people cannot handle the reality of life when worlds get turned upside down. Please treasure the few who stick around.

Moms at school will act funny around you. At first, I thought I had the plague because when I would walk in the moms would turn and walk the other way. It wasn't because I had the plague, it was because they don't know what to say. They cannot put themselves in my shoes and know what my heart feels. It is easier for them to ignore me. And that is ok.

Honesty! Be honest about your feelings. Be honest with your grief process. Be honest.

It is ok to be un-social. There is no need to force yourself. Even though your outer shell speaks that you are fine, your heart tells a different story.

It is perfectly normal to be sad & happy at the same time. You can still experience fun occasions & acknowledge your pain.

Time heals all wounds is false. This is a wound that will never heal until you are reunited with your child again. In time, you learn how to handle the pain. You learn to live with the pain.

You will find you again. It will be a different you. It will be a better you.

Life has a funny way of throwing curve balls and flipping upside down. This is your new normal. I am sorry this has happened to you. Understand you are not alone. We are all around feeling the same pain you feel.

With love,

Amanda.

Momma to Emma Eva Spaulding
12/17/15-12/18/17

Emma Eva: Our Journey with Trisomy 18: https://www.facebook.com/Emma-Eva-Our-Journey-with-Trisomy-18-535725723249338/

*LIFE HAS A FUNNY WAY OF THROWING
CURVE BALLS AND FLIPPING UPSIDE
DOWN. THIS IS YOUR NEW NORMAL. I
AM SORRY THIS HAS HAPPENED TO YOU.
UNDERSTAND YOU ARE NOT ALONE. WE
ARE ALL AROUND FEELING THE SAME PAIN
YOU FEEL.*

DEAR NEWLY BEREAVED MOTHER,

I know that you are probably feeling like the most isolated person in the entire world right now. Or, you may be bombarded with friends or family members who know someone that has been in your shoes and relentlessly try to induct you into this awful club. Yeah, we know they are trying to help… but who is ready to face the music at this point? Heck, in this life, who is ready to face the music at all… ever. You may be feeling a bubbling cauldron of things ranging from a desire to be close to people to wanting to crawl in a hole forever. You may be just wanting someone to call or text you hoping for the opportunity to ignore them instead of being ignored yourself. Maybe you want them all to just leave you alone.

What I am here to tell you is that all of these feelings are normal, expected, and even encouraged. You are going to experience things in a much different way than you ever have in your life. People along the way may be very supportive. I hope this is the case for you. They might celebrate with you and honor your grief and the love of your sweet baby or babies, gone too soon. I hope this is the case for you. Cherish these people as they are few and far between. People along the way may also change. They may decide that your grieving period is up. They may become uncomfortable with your grief and feel the need to intervene and make things "better" so they can have the "old you" back. Try to find the compassion for them within yourself that they struggle to find for you. It will bring you peace. However, don't be afraid to cut ties with people who are causing you more pain than you are already dealing with.

You don't have to go to the family get together. You don't have to attend the baby shower. You do not have to "like" or "comment" on the pictures of your Facebook friend's kids. You can even hide them. Go for it. It can be very relieving. Your responsibility now is surviving and making yourself comfortable. Even as the years have passed for me, I know all too well how difficult getting out of bed in the morning on some of those days can be. Give yourself credit for things you accomplish. Literally everything is much harder now than it was before. You are tough though, and you can do it.

I am not going to tell you that things start looking up or things get "better". That isn't for me to decide. Only you can decide what "better" means to you and what you are going to do to get there. Guess what? It's also ok to decide that you aren't "better" ever... just different. You are learning to mother a child that nobody can see or feel. If that isn't the hardest job in the world, I don't know what is. I have not yet achieved "better" for myself. I don't line anything with silver. My baby died. I miss him. I try to do my best to honor him. Does that make it "better"? Maybe some people see it that way.

My son's way too short life has left the world with his legacy. His very proud Mom is surviving… sort of, and helping others along the way in their path, because of him. Always because of him. That is how I mother him now and only you can decide for yourself how you are going to mother. However you do it, be brave, even if that means choosing to stay in your pajamas all day and watch Netflix. Even that can be a tough job in this new life. You can do it.

<3

Amber,
Jasper's Mom.

YOUR RESPONSIBILITY NOW IS SURVIVING AND MAKING YOURSELF COMFORTABLE. EVEN AS THE YEARS HAVE PASSED FOR ME, I KNOW ALL TOO WELL HOW DIFFICULT GETTING OUT OF BED IN THE MORNING ON SOME OF THOSE DAYS CAN BE. GIVE YOURSELF CREDIT FOR THINGS YOU ACCOMPLISH. LITERALLY EVERYTHING IS MUCH HARDER NOW THAN IT WAS BEFORE. YOU ARE TOUGH THOUGH, AND YOU CAN DO IT.

DEAR SWEET MOMMA,

Words cannot express how sorry I am that you are here. I am so sorry that you know the pain of saying goodbye to your child, that your heart is broken, and that your sweet baby is not here in your arms. I'm sorry that life has thrown this unbelievable curve ball your way and has turned your entire world upside down. I'm sorry for the triggers that you will face as you navigate this new life, the comments from family and friends that, although well-meaning, can be so hurtful. All of the anniversaries, birthdays, and moments that will now feel like such harsh reminders of what should have been. I'm sorry for your heart as you deal with the anxiety after loss that is so crushing to so many of us. I'm sorry for the sleepless nights, the tears that seem endless, the love that is pouring out of you, and the empty crib that just screams at you every time you manage the courage to walk into the nursery where your child should be sleeping.

Momma, sweet sweet Momma, my heart breaks for you. If I could take the pain away, I would in a second. I wish there was a magical formula to change your outcome, I truly do. All I can do is promise you, from one loss momma to another is although it seems far from possible you will find joy again. It will sting when it first happens and feel wrong, but, oh Momma, you will laugh again. You will smile again;

you will be able to breathe again. This won't mean that you've forgotten your child or that you no longer ache for them to be here with you. This doesn't erase the memory of your child or close the door on your grief. It simply means that when it's ready your heart will begin to mend. You'll still have dark days and you'll still miss your child with every fiber of your being, because they are your baby and they will always always be a part of you. This won't happen overnight, but slowly, one day at a time you will allow yourself to feel something other than just soul crushing pain again. And Momma, when you do, it's a powerful thing.

Look for your child in the beauty of this world. Find joy in each day because of the love you have for your baby. Remember that although you miss them dearly what a blessing it was to carry them, to hold them, to always love them.

One day at a time, Momma. Just take it one day at a time. And when the day overwhelms you, that's ok. Give yourself extra grace and please always remember that you are not alone. So many of us have walked this path before you and there is so much love and support here when your heart is ready. Please don't ever feel like no one understands, and please just remember that this life here on earth is only temporary. When our time is up, we will see our beautiful babies again and they will be in our arms for eternity. That day, when your baby is back in your arms, that will be the most beautiful of all days. But until then, keep living your life for your child. Make those memories and spread that joy for them and for you, Momma.

Forever your sister in loss,

Amelia Kowalisyn

Momma to Emma Rose (10.13.14-11.05.14) and four other sweet babies that I never met but hold in my heart.

Emma's Footprints: https://www.facebook.com/EmmaKsfootprints
Instagram: KowalisynKiddos

Amelia Kowalisyn is the mother of two sets of twins, Alex and Emma Rose (who is loving her family from up in Heaven), and Cameron and Christian. In addition to the loss of Emma at 23 days old, their family has experienced four miscarriages. Amelia and her husband Joe started their charity Emma's Footprints shortly after the loss of their daughter to provide support to neonatal intensive care unit (NICU) and bereaved parents. Amelia was also the director of outreach of the On Coming Alive Project and speaks openly and honestly about her journey as a bereaved parent. You can find Amelia on Facebook and Instagram.

LOOK FOR YOUR CHILD IN THE BEAUTY OF THIS WORLD. FIND JOY IN EACH DAY BECAUSE OF THE LOVE YOU HAVE FOR YOUR BABY. REMEMBER THAT ALTHOUGH YOU MISS THEM DEARLY WHAT A BLESSING IT WAS TO CARRY THEM, TO HOLD THEM, TO ALWAYS LOVE THEM.

DEAR MAMA,

My hearts holds yours close. With you, I wish it wasn't true. I wish your child were here to watch grow. I will always wish this for you. I will always wish this for me. The loss you feel is collective between every mom who has felt this pain, we carry it with you.

When we birth our babies, we take the largest risk of our life - to love someone far beyond ourselves. We create a life for our children before they are even here to experience it, beyond our bellies. We include them in who we are and all that we do before we can even hold them in our arms. We make plans for our future as our family grows.

It's a scary time and a beautiful time, full of anticipation.

Dreams.

Hopes.

Plans.

Expectations.

When our children are born, our hearts are full with an ever-expanding love that does not compare to anything else in the world. It overflows. And when the unfathomable happens, when our child dies, there is no tangible place to put that love. That love never goes away. In fact, I have found that my love has continued to grow and grow among the many years since my daughter left this life.

If you had told that my relationship with her would continue, I don't know that I would have believed you. I also don't know if it would have comforted me. But as the days turned to weeks, into months and now years, I found myself including her in the daily rituals of life that I wouldn't have imagined in the beginning.

I found the mornings to be the most difficult. The devastation and realization every morning that my daughter was no longer with me was cruel. I would drowsily stir between sleep and wake only to remember that my daughter had died and it would be as if I were learning the news all over again. It would take my breath away every single day.

When I would finally gather the courage and strength to get out of bed, I would walk to the window and raise its blinds. Even in the depths of my grief the sun would continue to rise and continue to cast it's light over my dark, devastated world.

"Good morning, world. Good morning, Ruthie." I would say, desperate to feel a connection with my daughter.

Years later, I still find myself opening the blinds in the morning and saying good morning to both the world and my only daughter, in similar fashion to how I greet my sleeping sons when they wake.

You see, in doing so, I feel my daughter's presence with me in every small action. She has become so ingrained in my body and in my soul that she is now part of everything I am and in everything I do, whether consciously or subconsciously.

When I make decisions now, whether life changing or inconsequential, I imagine the time of life when I learned my daughter's life would be brief. I find that when I answer with a similar sense of urgency that life is short and so precious, it helps to prioritize its importance.

Love.

Love was the only thing important when she was living.

Love continues to be the only thing important since her death.

If I remind myself of this principal, that love is all that matters, it makes all the big decisions much easier. It makes me feel close to my daughter, who infused my life with love from the moment I knew she existed.

The love that enveloped me when I was pregnant and the joy that I felt to hold her in my arms has fueled me for life. The time I shared with my daughter will never be enough, but my heart continues to overflow with love for her. I intend to live the rest of my life releasing that love to the world, to make beauty in what remains.

When the sun breaks and I see its rays rise up over the horizon, I remember to see beauty, I remember to feel love, and I always feel close to my daughter. I hope you can find beauty in what remains, whatever that might mean for you.

All my love, mama.

My heart holds you close always.

Love,

Amie

Ruthie Lou's mama
Ruthie Lou Lands (8/9/11-9/10/11)
www.amielandsauthor.com

LOVE.

LOVE WAS THE ONLY THING IMPORTANT WHEN SHE WAS LIVING.

LOVE CONTINUES TO BE THE ONLY THING IMPORTANT SINCE HER DEATH.

IF I REMIND MYSELF OF THIS PRINCIPAL, THAT LOVE IS ALL THAT MATTERS, IT MAKES ALL THE BIG DECISIONS MUCH EASIER. IT MAKES ME FEEL CLOSE TO MY DAUGHTER, WHO INFUSED MY LIFE WITH LOVE FROM THE MOMENT I KNEW SHE EXISTED.

DEAR BEAUTIFUL AND COURAGEOUS MOTHER,

We have never met, you and I, but I know what brings
you here. I see you. And, I recognize and understand the
heartbreak you're enduring.

I know you now understand that nothing in life is guaranteed
and not everything happens for a reason. Hideous things
can happen and these situations, despite all of our hopes
and beliefs, are entirely out of our control. There is no more
painful lesson to have to be learned in this world.

Our stories, our journeys, to motherhood are different yet
the same in so many ways. You and I, we have become aged
beyond our years in one single instant. We both have hearts
that yearn for children we can no longer physically hold. We
have been thrust into a club that no one wants or deserves
to be a part of, but here we stand. This club that welcomes
you with compassion and sees you with non-judgmental eyes
opens the door to a world full of shattered dreams, wishes,
and tears but, most importantly, hearts overflowing with
endless love.

I cannot lie to you, this grief we are in is ugly and agonizing.
Nothing in this world will hurt as much as this loss. It
hurts like hell and beyond. I've been there, I recognize your

anguish. There will be moments of darkness where all you want to do is drown in the pain, wishing you could simply succumb to the storm. This grief is terrifying as it creeps deep into the corners of your heart, unable to be outrun. Please, sweet Mother, know that it is alright to embrace the pain, the anger, the guilt, the resentment, the tears and screams. It is the price we pay for a love so infinite and beautiful that it eclipses the stars. Ours is a love so powerful that it stretches out with invisible arms and holds your baby from afar.

It is exhausting and I know you are tired, however, I also know you will continue to battle the waves and the wind, even when you are so broken you believe you no longer can. You will continue to take one breath at a time, one step, then another. I know this. I know this because you will want to be the best mother you can be to your child. In the midst of utter, spiraling darkness you will still want to be strong for them, yearning to make them proud. You will find the strength, the strength that only comes with being a mother. Even if all you can do is manage to survive for a minute, an hour, a day, you do it because you are still a mom.

I understand the if's and why's that race continuously through your mind. I know what it's like to fall apart at every turn, to be called strong when all you feel is shattered and wanting nothing more than to be normal. I know what it's like to want to scream and cry at everyone around you in an effort to try and get them to understand one ounce of your pain. To try to get them to say your child's name just so you can hear it. . .to hear how beautiful it sounds.

There will be many individuals that won't understand, and relationships will be challenged and frayed to the point of breaking. Family, friends and strangers will spew out the well-intentioned platitudes that cut through your heart like a knife and reopen wounds. Don't listen to those that insist your grief isn't valid or justified. Don't believe them when they paint your child as a dark spot on your past or tell you that you're grieving wrong. Nothing will replace your missing child and no one else is allowed to dictate how you mourn. You, and only you, will find what you need to do to love, honor, celebrate and protect your precious baby's memory. Whether you shout their name from the rooftops or clutch and keep them silently close to your heart, there is no wrong way to love.

I know the fear you carry of the future. The fear of a lifetime of emptiness and forever longing for the return of the missing piece of your heart. I know how scary the promise of lighter days are when you want nothing more than to feel the pain in order to remain closer to them. The fear of living too long in sadness but the challenge of imagining an existence with happiness and joy - the guilt of life continuously moving forward without them. I know your desire to will time to stop so you don't have to see others continue to live as if nothing has changed; as if your little one didn't matter. They do matter! Your child was your future and still is. Your angel has left their mark on this world, your family, and nothing can ever change that.

I can't promise much, but I can promise you are loved and your child is loved and will always be remembered. I know you will work and continue to strive daily to weave this delicate balance of love and loss into a new world filled with moments of gentle grace and beautiful dreams. Remember, your baby is never far from your side, nuzzling your cheek when you cry and hugging you at night while you sleep. You will never forget your precious child and your love for them will never fade. Even in moments when you are swept up in your "new normal", your heart will remember. Your heart will always carry them and keep them safe until you are reunited and able to hold them again. . .this time, never to let them go.

With love,

Amy Cirksena

Savannah Grace Cirksena

PLEASE, SWEET MOTHER, KNOW THAT IT IS ALRIGHT TO EMBRACE THE PAIN, THE ANGER, THE GUILT, THE RESENTMENT, THE TEARS AND SCREAMS. IT IS THE PRICE WE PAY FOR A LOVE SO INFINITE AND BEAUTIFUL THAT IT ECLIPSES THE STARS. OURS IS A LOVE SO POWERFUL THAT IT STRETCHES OUT WITH INVISIBLE ARMS AND HOLDS YOUR BABY FROM AFAR.

On April 12th, 2004 at 6:13am Anna Irene Hermodson Kjorlien was born still. She was born in the 36th week of pregnancy, 33 days from her expected due date. She was 19 ½ inches and weighed 6 pounds. Anna had 10 perfect fingers, 10 perfect toes, dark, curly, brown hair, Mommy's head, Daddy's chin, a cute, button nose, chubby cheeks, pouty mouth, and soft, pink skin.

It was the worst day of my life, and it was the best day of my life.

My water broke around midnight on the 12th of April. There was a bit of a scramble to get the hospital. We had not packed a hospital bag, and I had no clue prior to that moment that I was going into labor. It was a surreal moment, and one that right from the start of it all felt like an out-of-body experience. Shortly after arrival at the hospital, I was greeted by Tweetie, a nurse who led our labor and delivery classes. When Tweetie put a monitor on my belly, it revealed the devastating news that there was no signs of life in Anna.

And somehow, I just knew she was gone before Tweetie told me so. And somehow, I was filled with nothing but calm, determination, and strength. I was going to do the last thing on Earth that I would do for my daughter... give birth to her. Out of the worst thing that can happen to a parent, I was going to do something good. I was going to do that because of, and for her. She deserved nothing less than that.

Anna was born just as the sun was rising that day. It was also the day that Minnesota came to life after a long winter. The air was warm, the birds sang, bulbs were blooming, and the first leaves started to pop on the trees and bushes in the woods behind our house. In the weeks to come, babies of all kinds came into the world. Baby deer, fox, birds, and rabbits in our yard. Baby cows, horses, goats, and chickens in the farm yards surrounding our town. Babies of neighbors, friends, and family were also born. Each birth a bittersweet reminder of life's continuance, and of death's devastating blow.

Spring has been a yearly reminder of the worst day of my life. It is also a comforting reminder of the best day of my life.

Just as there are countless ways to grieve a loss, there are countless ways to cope with loss. From the earliest weeks after Anna's birth until now, I have focused on the great gifts that Anna brought to me in her short time on Earth. I never felt more alive than the time in which I carried Anna – I felt physically wonderful, I was completely happy, and felt a great deal of hope. I never felt stronger than I did in the few hours it took to deliver her. And though her life was far too short, I couldn't be more proud of the daughter who has touched my life, and countless other lives, over the course of the last thirteen years since her birth.

In 2011, Salon posted the following question to its website,
"What, if anything, has grief taught you?" If I could choose
one answer it would be that grief taught me how to live…
really live. It was my wake-up call to let "control" go, really
experience the here and now moment, and pay attention to
what matters to me in this world. When I'm really living life,
I am constantly aware that I always have a choice… there is
always something I can do that is good for me and for others.
I am aware that what matters most to me are the connections
that I have with my friends, my family, my community,
and people across the world. I pay more attention to the
people around me, pick up on what they need, have more
compassion for and listen to them better (and I do the same
things for myself). I don't spend time asking, "why," or
being consumed with questions of "what ifs and should've/
would've/could've." I lost so much when my daughter died,
but I also gained so much, too. I'm truly grateful for that gift
born out of grief. It's the best thing that has happened in my
life. And none of it would have been possible without Anna.

DEAREST ANNA,

Our joys have been and will continue to be greater,

Our love has been and will continue to be deeper,

Our life has been and will continue to be fuller,

Because we shared your moment.

What we remember of you will live on forever.

Love,

Mommy and Daddy

Amy Hermodson,
Mother to Anna Irene

AND THOUGH HER LIFE WAS FAR TOO SHORT, I COULDN'T BE MORE PROUD OF THE DAUGHTER WHO HAS TOUCHED MY LIFE, AND COUNTLESS OTHER LIVES, OVER THE COURSE OF THE LAST THIRTEEN YEARS SINCE HER BIRTH.

DEAR STRONG MOMMA,

I am so sorry for the loss of your sweet child. It is a pain that I am all too familiar with and one that no one should ever have to experience. You will hear quite frequently throughout your journey the phrase "there are no words." Unfortunately, this statement is true. There really are no words to make this loss any better and no words that can fix what happened to you and your baby. The most important thing to remember is that this event happened TO you. You did not cause this to happen to your precious child.

It is a loss that you will carry with you every day for the rest of your life. You will never "move on." That statement implies getting over the loss and putting it in the past. However, I can tell you that you will be able to move forward. You will be able to smile again. It will feel very strange at first and you will probably feel guilty about it. I know I did and that's okay. You think to yourself, "How can I be happy and smiling when I just lost my child?!" Trust me, I get it. But at some point, there will be something that makes you smile. Embrace it. Those moments are few and far between, so cherish them when they happen.

There is no right way to grieve the loss of your baby. You are not simply grieving the loss of them, but the life you dreamed of having with your child. Certain days will be harder than others. Holidays will now be painted with a tinge of sadness at the piece missing from your life. There is no place that is safe from the reminder of what you lost. Emotional triggers will be everywhere. The grocery store becomes a mine field of mothers with their children. Commercials on television are plagued with images of babies and they don't even have to be selling baby products! A familiar song could send you on the verge of an emotional breakdown. All of these triggers will cause a reaction - anger, sadness, frustration, bitterness, etc., but that is okay. You are grieving an immense loss and you have the right to feel however you feel!

Do what you need to in order to feel close to your child - sleep with their blanket, snuggle their teddy bear, fill your home with photos of your precious baby. Do not let the opinions of others color how you parent your child after they are gone. Because that is what you are doing, you are parenting your child. Your way is just different from others because your child isn't with you.

Most importantly, know that you are not alone in this loss. There are so many members of this horrible "club" and we are all here for you. The strongest people you will ever meet in your life are the mothers and fathers that exist in this community, bound together by loss. You are strong. You may not feel that way, but you are. You suffered the loss of a child and you are still here. It takes incredible strength to get out of bed each day and trudge on. You are a mother and you are a strong one, don't ever forget that.

With Love,

Amy Lied

Asher's Mommy 2/19/17
https://doggiebagsnotdiaperbags.wordpress.com/

*THE MOST IMPORTANT THING TO
REMEMBER IS THAT THIS EVENT
HAPPENED TO YOU. YOU DID NOT CAUSE
THIS TO HAPPEN TO YOUR PRECIOUS
CHILD.*

HELLO MAMA,

My heart breaks at the thought of you reading this. No one should know this pain, and I wish we weren't meeting over these pages. I wish we had instead met at the park, with each of us pushing our babies in their stroller. Things would feel happier and lighter. I am so sorry you find yourself on this journey of loss.

I remember the fog of those first weeks after losing our daughter. Nothing seemed real, and I found myself feeling hollow. As time passed, I began to realize I'd lost so much more than my little girl. The innocence and hope of pregnancy was gone. As were the smile and joy that had once been my constant companions. Everything I thought I had known was ripped from my soul. I wondered if I would ever feel whole again.

As this path continues to unfold before me, I'm starting to accept that I'll never be the same person I was before. Maybe it's the same for you. I've had my heart broken, my soul torn, and the life I knew has been shattered. I think a lot of people who haven't experienced grief themselves expect us to go back to who we were before loss. But that's impossible. Even the vase that has been glued back together will still have cracks. The cracks might look invisible to some, while others might not be able to stand their appearance. But there will always be someone who can appreciate their beauty.

And just like that vase, you are beautiful. I can see the pain that hides behind your smile, and I know it's a pain born out of the immense love you have for your child. I can think of few things more beautiful than that.

There are times I wish none of this had happened, or that I didn't know this pain. But in many ways, I find myself grateful for it too. The lifetime of loving her is so much greater than the sorrow of her death. I would relive the loss over and over again just to know our daughter. The beauty of this entire experience can be found in my love for her. The same beauty is in yours too - don't forget to look for it.

Always thinking of you,

Anna

Lillian's Mom
Instagram: @letterstolilllian
Blog: http://www.letterstolilllianblig.com

THE LIFETIME OF LOVING HER IS SO MUCH GREATER THAN THE SORROW OF HER DEATH. I WOULD RELIVE THE LOSS OVER AND OVER AGAIN JUST TO KNOW OUR DAUGHTER. THE BEAUTY OF THIS ENTIRE EXPERIENCE CAN BE FOUND IN MY LOVE FOR HER. THE SAME BEAUTY IS IN YOURS TOO - DON'T FORGET TO LOOK FOR IT.

OH, SWEET MOMMA,

First, I am so, SO sorry you are here.

This is a horrible nightmare we are living in. I say "we" because you are not alone. We are here, all of us. And I know that still doesn't make this any easier.

I became a mommy of an angel on June 25, 2016 when my husband Hank and I saw our beautiful daughter in the delivery room. That day rocked our world forever.

My husband and I had been trying for almost 4 years to get pregnant. We had started to lose hope. I was emotionally exhausted from the side effects and my hormones fluctuating. So, after discussing every option, we had decided to postpone our baby dreams in August of 2015. To our surprise, we found out we were expecting in January of 2016.

God had fulfilled our hopes and dreams. We were elated and couldn't wait to tell our friends and family.

I had the most amazing pregnancy. Well, besides a little nausea that kept me from eating, but I also lost some weight, which was another bonus to carrying this baby. I was so happy I was carrying life within me. Everything was wonderful... until it wasn't.

I had noticed that my darling ballerina, as we called her since she was always dancing on my bladder, hadn't been active. On my way to work on June 23rd, I called my husband and told him I was just going to go get checked out. I figured she had finally just rotated and was laying on her side. I had no doubt that she was okay.

I had three nurses come in to try to find her heartbeat. They were having trouble and said it was because the machine they were using wasn't great at picking up a heartbeat at 21-22 weeks; but swore they heard her moving around. Thankfully my doctor was at the hospital delivering another baby and ordered an ultrasound for me.

That was the first time I had some doubts, but I stayed positive for myself and my husband. I hadn't had one negative thought. I hadn't shed one tear. I hadn't even mentioned the possibility of my baby being dead.

That was until the doctor came in ten minutes later. As soon as my husband saw her face he said, "this isn't good." She had been crying and she came over to us and said the dreaded words to any expecting parent.

"They can't find the heartbeat."

She rechecked herself and confirmed the horrible news. I remember she turned the machine off, turned to us, and said "I'm sorry" as she leaned in to hug us. She knew this was our first, and only child. She knew how hard we had worked for this child, and prayed for this child. Our doctor had been through it all with us, and she said that it felt like she lost her baby too. We cried and prayed, and I apologized to Hank because I just knew this was my fault.

Then, after a few minutes of feeling crushed there was a calming peacefulness about everything. It could have only been because of the presence of God in that room.

Hank and I had given everything over to God months before this ugly day. We knew that no matter what had happened or what was to come in this pregnancy, He would have us in His arms. We felt God there. We knew He was the one breathing peace and love into our lungs. Looking back now I feel like He was the only reason I was still breathing. He never left us.

Trust is the feeling of security you have when your feet are solidly planted on a Rock that towers high above all your enemies. That Rock is also a place of safety where you can find secure refuge and shelter. Psalm 61:3-4

Don't get me wrong, although we were pressing into our faith, we were still hurting badly. There were moments we would cry until we couldn't breathe. We would hold each other. I would continue to apologize to Hank. I just knew if I hadn't taken that flight to Virginia a couple of weeks before, or if I hadn't gone on that beach ride that was so bumpy, she would still be with us. All the irrational thoughts crept into my mind. I knew deep down I couldn't have done anything to save our beautiful baby girl. Please, Momma, know this is not your fault and you did all you could for your baby.

Our daughter, Brooklynn Elyse Allen, was born still on June 25, 2016, when I was almost 22 weeks' gestation due to an umbilical cord accident. We were one of the couples who could find out exactly what had caused our little one to pass too soon. If you are a momma who didn't get that answer and closure, my heart hurts even more for you. I know that knowing what caused the death of your beloved wouldn't make it any easier. Still, the not knowing would make it so much worse on me personally. I, again, am SO very sorry.

Brooklynn was beautiful! We were able to hold her, kiss her, read her a book, and take pictures with her. Our friends and family came and shared the joyous moment with us, and the sorrow of knowing we wouldn't be taking her home. A moment was exactly what it was, and it wasn't long enough.

Dearest Momma, I know this is absolutely devastating, soul crushing, and earth- shattering. I wish you weren't reading this. I wish you weren't part of this "club," but I'm glad that I can be here to walk through it with you. Even if I'm not physically there with you, please know I am thinking about you and praying for you every day.

You are strong. You are brave. You will make it through this.

I know your heart is broken. I wish so much that I could take this away from you. I wish I could take away your pain and make you whole again.

Whether you've lost your child at 6 weeks or 21 weeks, at full term, or even after giving birth, a 3-year-old, or a 30-year-old, you have lost your child. You have lost a part of you.

Just remember to breathe. Don't hide your grief, let it go. Cry, scream, curse, cry some more, pray, and never hide your grief. Do what heals you.

Dear Momma, remember that you are always on my mind. I hope this letter offers even a tiny bit of comfort to you.

You are not alone.
You will be okay. We are all here for you.

With love,

Ashley

Brooklynn's Mommy xxx

*I KNEW DEEP DOWN I COULDN'T HAVE
DONE ANYTHING TO SAVE OUR BEAUTIFUL
BABY GIRL. PLEASE, MOMMA, KNOW THIS
IS NOT YOUR FAULT AND YOU DID ALL YOU
COULD FOR YOUR BABY.*

DEAREST MAMA,

I know you have just entered into a new world. One that can be so cruel, dark and lonely. But that is why I am here. To share with you that you are not alone and all of us are with you.

While we may all be at different parts of the journey of motherhood and loss, we are all on the same path together. So from my mother's heart to yours, I want to pass along a few things that I have learned from being Lillian's mommy

First that is to make sure that you know, that you know, that you know - YOU ARE A MOTHER. MOM. MOMMY. Say it with me, "I am a mommy." Even if you don't feel like it. Even if the world doesn't see it or acknowledge it because many just don't fully understand. That's who you are now. As your arms ache to hold your little one(s) know that you are still a mommy. You will always and forever remain a mommy. Say it as often as you need until it echoes into your heart and take root. Remind yourself often. You are a mother. A brave one. Learning to love your little one from here.

Secondly, there is nothing you could have done. You couldn't have done any more. I know it doesn't make sense and you may blame yourself or even your own body. Be gentle with you. It wasn't your fault. It never was and it never will be. So much is lost already, try not to lose yourself in this lie. You did all you could with what you knew. It's ok, Mama, to feel this way but don't remain here for too long. It's not a place to stay. Release it. And know you are not to blame. . .ever. This is something I needed to do so much. Even still.

If no one else will celebrate and honor my Lily, I will. I give you permission to celebrate and honor your little one(s). Go ahead and buy that toy. Hang that stocking with the rest of the kids'. Have a cake and sing happy birthday each year if you desire. Release balloons. Sign their precious name with the rest of the family on cards. Teach brothers and sisters about their sibling. It's ok to include them, after all they are still part of your family. Honor them however you feel is right no matter how silly it may seem to the outside world. It's worth it. I promise.

Such a great burden was lifted the day my dear friend said this, "It's ok to think that. It's normal." Those were the words I needed to hear so desperately. How you feel or what you're thinking is probably normal considering all you have experienced. It's normal to feel overwhelmed. It's normal to not have energy. It's normal to cry. Be angry. To withdraw. To scream. To lose interest in things you once enjoyed. It's even normal to feel like you're going crazy or like you might never laugh again. It's ok to go to counseling. It's ok to need help.

It's ok, dear Mama. It's hard and you're doing a good job just learning how to be and live in this "new normal." Again, be gentle with yourself and allow your heart to grieve. Let that grief come out however you need to and take the time to let all your pain come forth. Of course it hurts - a piece of your heart isn't here with you.

And last but not least; love them loudly and wildly. Love is what compels you to honor your baby, to include them. Love is also the reason you miss them so much and long to have them in your arms. I have learned myself that even though your baby is no longer here physically, that does not mean you love them any less. Love goes beyond the grave. It is that fierce. It is that strong. It is that powerful. That love will keep you connected to them. How, I can't explain it but it will. So love big and love loud. For them. Shout it from the rooftops. And may it compel you to do something to help other mamas like you or to honor little ones like ours. Love will make a way for you to live again. To smile again. And to carry them inside your heart forever.

Oh sweet Mama, how I wish I could hug you, say your baby's name and listen to you tell the story of their life. No matter how brief - please understand that they have made a mark on this world. They have made a difference just by being them! By coming into the world. Your world!

May you hold on to these truths when the nights seem so long and the days are dark and grim. Until the light shines again, may you find comfort in knowing you are not alone. Comfort in knowing that even though you may no longer see them, they are still yours and you are - and always will be - their mommy. And may you find comfort in the love you share with them. Until we see our "littles" again...

Lillian's mommy,

Bethany Stewart

Forever a part of me–
Lillian Ember Stewart (my first child)
Born into heaven on 11/23/13
She has taught me more about love and motherhood then I ever thought was possible and she continues to teach me daily. I love you so much so my Lily.

My blog :
EmbersandArrows

*YOU WILL ALWAYS AND FOREVER REMAIN
A MOMMY. SAY IT AS OFTEN AS YOU NEED
UNTIL IT ECHOES INTO YOUR HEART AND
TAKE ROOT. REMIND YOURSELF OFTEN.
YOU ARE A MOTHER. A BRAVE ONE.
LEARNING TO LOVE YOUR LITTLE ONE
FROM HERE.*

MY DEAR FELLOW LOSS MAMA,

My heart hurts so much to be writing to you. The pain is so awful and I hate that you too have known this pain. There are no words that can adequately describe how terrible it is to lose a child.

I want to tell you that you are strong. Every day when you get up, you are strong. When you face each day, each event, each milestone with such important people in your life missing, you are strong.

You are not alone. I want you to know that. Know that when you are curled up in a ball and crying your eyes out. Know that when you wish you could cry, but it feels like your tears are all spent. Know that when you don't recognize yourself in the mirror. Know that when you have a good day, when you find yourself laughing. Know that when you enjoy a moment. You are not alone.

For me, one of the hardest things is feeling like I am the only one who cares. The only one who knows. The only one who loves my children in heaven. If no one in your life acknowledges your child or children, I'm sorry. I'm so sorry. Your babies deserve to be known and loved. Try to remember too, that most likely there are people in your life who do care. They just don't know what to say or how to say it. No one can feel your loss as deeply as you can, because you were the mama. You knew your child better than anyone. You will always have that special bond with your child.

Those feelings you feel? They are real. They are normal. Your baby mattered. Because their life was real. Because this baby was not just a pregnancy, it was not a potential baby, it was a child. A person. Your unique, precious, wonderful child. And they are loved. So loved.

There is no getting over this loss. There is no moving on. There is only moving forward. Don't be afraid to speak of your children. Others might not, but you can. I love being able to speak my son's name, and talk about my other babies as if they were my children. Because they are. Some people don't get that, but that is ok. I talk about them because they are my children as much as my living 4 year old is. I talk about them because I am insanely proud of them and I love them so immensely.

If you're like me, you have probably asked some pretty gut-wrenching questions. Chief of which is probably along the lines of, "Why?" And ...I don't know. I have asked that so many times. There may or may not be a medical reason. And while there may be some comfort in a medical reason, it doesn't really answer the question. Why did this happen? Why did my child/ren have to die? I have wrestled with some intense theological questions and I will be honest when I say it has challenged my view of God. I have about one hundred questions that all end in "I don't know."

"For you formed my inward parts;
you knitted me together in my mother's womb.
I praise you, for I am fearfully and wonderfully made.
Wonderful are your works;
my soul knows it very well.
My frame was not hidden from you,
when I was being made in secret,
intricately woven in the depths of the earth.
Your eyes saw my unformed substance;
in your book were written, every one of them,
the days that were formed for me,
when as yet there were none of them."
Psalm 139:13-16

I love that passage, because it reminds me of how precious my children, and all unborn children are, to God. Our three children, and your children, are in heaven right now. And their souls know very well how wonderful are His works. They are dancing and praising and worshiping. Right at this very moment, their joy is unspeakable. They know no tears and no pain. They are loved and cherished by the King of Kings.

This pain sometimes feels unbearable. But I am reminded that Jesus conquered death. It is for this reason, for this awful repercussion of living in a fallen world, it is for the death of our children, it is for sin, that Jesus died. He is the Victor. Someday all will be put right.

Yes, you are strong. No mother should ever have to say good-bye to her child. I hope you know, on your awful days and your not-as-awful days and even on your good days, that you are surrounded (hopefully in person, but definitely in thought and spirit) by a multitude of women who have been through the same. I wish we could sit down together in person. I wish I could hear about your wonderful precious child. I wish I could tell you about my children. They are all so special and loved.

You are loved.

—Bonnie

Mother of a precious 4 year old boy on earth
Precious baby lost at 6 weeks
Precious baby lost at 6 weeks
Caden Jusa, precious boy lost at 16 weeks

www.lifewithyou1222.com

I WISH WE COULD SIT DOWN TOGETHER IN PERSON. I WISH I COULD HEAR ABOUT YOUR WONDERFUL PRECIOUS CHILD. I WISH I COULD TELL YOU ABOUT MY CHILDREN. THEY ARE ALL SO SPECIAL AND LOVED.

YOU ARE LOVED.

DEAR MOTHER,

I am sorry to welcome you to this group, whether your child was fully grown or had not yet had the chance to grow. I am sorry. I am sorry you are part of this circle. This circle full of parents who do not wish to be here. The club where the membership cost is high and the stakes are everlasting.

In late 2008, I was driving home late at night and I was listening to talkback radio, a series called Conversations with Richard Fielder. He was speaking to a woman, Emma McLeod. She had found out her baby had died and had gone home for the night, come back to hospital and given birth to a little girl. One of the midwives asked if she wanted to tell anyone. She didn't know what to say so she called a close friend and said the baby had arrived and then dropped the bombshell, that her daughter was a stillborn. She went on to found the Stillborn Foundation Australia. At the time, I remember feeling so much sympathy for her, at the loss and senselessness of it all. I can now say I truly understand and empathize with Emma.

I was 37 weeks and four days pregnant with my first child. It was a straight forward pregnancy; with the typical morning sickness and fatigue. But working long hours as a registered nurse in a busy intensive care unit always takes its toll. If anything, my pregnancy made me less irritable with most people. I seemed to have a lot of anxiety throughout the pregnancy and as my mother says first time mothers are a different species. My husband, Joe, is in the Navy and was based out of Sydney for most of the pregnancy and missed a few things but with the wonders of modern technology he was as involved as could be. Joe had made a few midwife and obstetrician appointments and we were able to set up the nursery together. I was living in Western Australia, where our families are based.

Joe and I had decided not to find out the gender of our baby. I had seen my obstetrician on a Thursday and everything looked great and he was happy, that the baby was growing well and moving around enough. The next day I was travelling about 400km north to my childhood hometown for my brother-in-law's 30th birthday, the baby's movements were quiet during the car ride, but this was normal. I picked one of my brothers up on the way, it was nice to have company for a 5-hour drive.

I arrived in my hometown, settled in, and caught up with family. That night I dropped my mum off at the hospital, where she works as a nurse, for a night shift. I caught up with a friend I had not seen for around 12 months. I had a sense of foreboding, but put it back to the anxiety I had had for most of the pregnancy. I had spoken to Joe and told him to enjoy a night on the drink with his navy friends as this opportunity may not come around again anytime soon.

My mum called at 0100, to say she was unwell and ask me if could I pick her up. I went in and got her. Once at home I asked her to call the hospital and tell them I was coming in, the anxiety could not be shaken and I wanted to be checked out as the baby's movements seem to have stopped. I arrived at the hospital and was taken up into the assessment room of to the labour ward. The midwife tried to find a heartbeat with the CTG and couldn't find anything. Another midwife from the ward came and tried, she could not find a heartbeat either. This was the moment I knew.

The midwives said they would do an ultrasound to see where that baby's head was so they knew they were looking in the right place. I said that baby was head down when I saw my obstetrician yesterday and what way the baby had been facing. With one midwife on one side of the bed and the other midwife with the ultrasound. On Saturday morning at 3:45am, over me they shared that look. As a nurse I know that look, it is a look of devastation and how do I deliver the worst news to this person. I spoke first and stated that they couldn't find a heartbeat and I understood the reality of my situation. The midwives said they were the experts and would have to call the doctor in. My mum came to join me and we went through the formal bloods and ultrasound. In the meantime, I was trying to contact Joe and tell him. His phone had died and at 5:00 he called me. I had to make the hardest sentence in my life, "I'm sorry Joe, the baby has died, they can't find a heartbeat." Joe made arrangements to come back to Western Australia.

At 6:30, Mum and I returned home and began to deliver the news to one of my sisters, my brother and my Dad. Dad, Mum and I started to organise the trip to go back to Perth. I rang my other sister and brother, they were travelling from Perth for the party. It was organised so that my siblings would be together and I could have my parents for the journey ahead.

We made the road trip to Perth, picked up Joe and went to the hospital. We were admitted at around 5pm. We did not see any doctors until around 8:30pm. The doctors made their apologies and I said I had heard the emergency bells and there were women they could help, there was nothing more that could be done for me. We underwent amniocentesis, which to this day remains the most traumatic part of my story. As Joe and I walked Mum and Dad to their car that night, we spotted a little owl in a paperbark tree. My Dad told me later that the owl had followed my voice wherever I walked under the tree.

The next day Sunday 28/08 I was induced and at 4:09pm I gave birth to a baby boy. We named him William Michael Joseph. He was beautiful, born still but still perfect. Mum and Joe gave him his first bath and we began the procession of family and friends visiting.

The time in hospital was a little bubble away from reality, from the stark reality that we were to return home to. Joe, William and I had family time together, small moments, such as making hand and feet prints and walking William to the morgue when Joe and I were discharged. We returned home and began to plan a funeral, this was made an easy process by family rallying together and help where they could. The funeral was a week later and will remain one of the most memorable days of my life. Over 120 people attended, for a baby no one has met and this blew me away.

During my grieving journey, there has been moments of devastation and misery, but also moments of happiness and joy. Often, they occur alongside one another, hand in hand. Some days the best I have to offer is I am breathing and I get myself out of bed. On other days the sky is the limit. It has been a process of merging myself into a role I would not wish upon anyone, being an invisible mother.

I look back to the conversation I had listened to in 2008, I get it. I know how Emma felt. I am there, I am living it now.

Emma McLeod went on to change things in a big way. My plan is to change things in a small way, one day at a time. I share my son William openly, with anyone who will listen. Because he was here, even from the briefest of times. I don't plan to change the world, but if I change one person's day that's enough for me.

The greatest support and resources I have found comes from Nathalie Himmerlich and her page the Grieving Parents Support Network. Annually she runs an event called "May We All Heal," focused on creative healing with word prompts, one for each day of May. I participated this year and found myself in a solace with my grief. I have discovered ways of functioning with my grief and making it part of me and a plot line of my story, instead of being the story itself.

At William's funeral, I said "If ever there is a tomorrow we are not together there is something you must remember. You are braver than you believe and stronger than you seem and smarter than you think. But the most important thing is ever if we are apart I will always be with you".

My dear mother, remember this, you have gotten this far and you can go the distance.

Love,

Carolyn

Mother to William Michael Joseph

EMMA MCLEOD WENT ON TO CHANGE THINGS IN A BIG WAY. MY PLAN IS TO CHANGE THINGS IN A SMALL WAY, ONE DAY AT A TIME. I SHARE MY SON WILLIAM OPENLY, WITH ANYONE WHO WILL LISTEN. BECAUSE HE WAS HERE, EVEN FROM THE BRIEFEST OF TIMES. I DON'T PLAN TO CHANGE THE WORLD, BUT IF I CHANGE ONE PERSON'S DAY THAT'S ENOUGH FOR ME.

DEAR FELLOW LOSS MOM,

Recently I left a parking garage and as I drove off, it hit me again how it felt the day I left the hospital empty handed. It's been nearly four years and yet I remembered that fresh, unbearable pain and realization that my life was drastically altered from how I pictured it would be.

My son Joel passed away two days after he was born. We left the hospital the same day he died; our bags packed up and our NICU ID bracelet still on our wrists. There was no baby carrier being used in the back seat of our car. My partner drove and I sat motionless in the front passenger seat - the silence of the car was deafening.

When we approached the parking garage attendant so we could pay and exit, he smiled and asked "New parents? Taking the baby home?" I froze in horror as this was the first time I had been confronted with the harsh reality that I was a childless mother. Joel's dad replied quietly, "No, our baby passed away." The attendant's face showed his regret for his comment and he told us "no charge for you today" while raising the bar so we could drive off.

It was the longest drive home as tears rolled down my face. I was still dealing with what my future now was. Just months before I had envisioned this task of taking my baby home from the hospital as being his first ever car ride. Now I realized that I would never drive him anywhere in a car.

That was the "first" of the many "baby less firsts" I experienced - which honestly, I would have rather missed out on. When I returned to the workforce not long after my son's funeral, I cried because I realized I would never drop him off at daycare. When I packed up the belongings I had gotten for my son, I realized I would never wash his little baby outfits or clean up after him. While grocery shopping in the store, I realized I wouldn't coo and smile at him riding in the shopping cart while putting groceries in the basket.

This was a very painful realization to accept. To accept my son was never going to be here to experience life. With time, I adjusted to this being my lot in life and pushed on through the numbness. There were days I didn't think I could accept that this was my reality - but I kept moving forward, slowly and painfully. Joel wouldn't want me to give up.

After a while I started to focused on what time I did have with my son while I was pregnant and when he was born, and be grateful for it. There is still frequently a twinge of sadness over "what might have been" but I've learned to focus on what I had. And if I had to do it all over again, I would still want that time with Joel. Because while I missed out on so many firsts - I got to be his mother and nothing could ever take that away. Forever, I will be Joel's mother, the one who loved him first. And that has become enough.

Accept that you won't get the life you planned to have with your child, work through the hurt and unfairness of it all, and know that your child knew and felt your love. You don't journey alone - many of us also have walked this path and shared in this pain.

Wishing you much strength during this difficult time,

Chrissy

Mother to Joel David

*AND IF I HAD TO DO IT ALL OVER AGAIN,
I WOULD STILL WANT THAT TIME WITH
JOEL. BECAUSE WHILE I MISSED OUT
ON SO MANY FIRSTS - I GOT TO BE HIS
MOTHER AND NOTHING COULD EVER TAKE
THAT AWAY. FOREVER, I WILL BE JOEL'S
MOTHER, THE ONE WHO LOVED HIM
FIRST. AND THAT HAS BECOME ENOUGH.*

DEAR MOTHER - SISTER,

This is a letter I never thought I'd be writing; nor is it something that you'd ever thought to receive. Of all the gifts in the world, apart from your child, you get this letter instead. I can relate.

I can give you words of advice, but by now you have heard all the uplifting words that, if you are like me, were received deflated. I got tired of hearing others' attempts to support me because their choice of words was all too common. I wanted words filled with personal from-the-bottom-of-their-heart meaning. So that is what you'll receive from me, from-the-bottom-of-my-heart advice.

I'm writing this letter just two years after my beloved son's quick entrance into another paradise. It is a place where I can't see him; a place where only he knows why he went. I believe in the intangible world; where spirits soar and angels guide. Where we cannot see those we love, but can feel their presence.

I can remember waking up several times a day looking into the mirror and crying my heart out; then going back to bed to wake and do it again. By his one year angel-versary, I had established a ritual of visiting his gravesite twice weekly. Between work and other responsibilities, this time was my commitment to my son. A way to show him how much I cared for him. By two years, I had created different ways to spend time with my son. Now every time I want to feel close to him, I connect by either walking trails, sitting on my bench, or practicing meditations.

These trails are where I walked when he was in womb. When I walk, I sometimes feel his presence when a strong wind blows through the trees even though the day is calm. When I sit on a bench in my backyard, he shows me cloud art that reminds me of him. And once when I was having a bad day, out of nowhere a blue butterfly glided across my path as if he were saying, "I'm right here by your side."

Not everyone witnesses or believes these manifestations because we live within the seeing dimension. Many have forgotten how to feel, to sense, to know. You may not believe in these thoughts, or maybe you're open to it. And maybe you need something to help you believe. Let this letter be it, let it encourage you to recognize the presence of your child. Just close your eyes and feel the sensations surrounding you. After awhile, you'll begin to feel or even see the same sensations occurring time and time again. Whether it may be a tingling on your face, a blue butterfly fluttering about, a special song on the radio, or recurring pennies on the ground. These are not coincidences; these are the ways loved ones try to communicate with us.

And if you find yourself doubting my advice, ask yourself if you are one to follow the saying, "seeing is believing." Because mother-sister, this is furthest from the truth.

So, find a way to communicate and listen to your loved one daily. Even if you get discouraged, your child is listening when you speak. Those intimate conversations you quietly have with your child are heard. You know, the ones when you pour your heart, tears, and confusion out to anyone, any being that will hear your angst and plea.

You may be able to hear or feel a response blowing through the trees, parting through the clouds, or appearing right in front of you. Keep that connection going because your child is waiting to have that unimagined relationship with you, unlike any other one you'll have. And that, my mother-sister, is the gift you never dreamed of having.

With empathy and sincerity,

Christine Markowski

Mother to Lolo Markowski,

I attribute my healing to the Japanese healing art called Reiki, and I have started a business helping others such as we.

www.BellinghamReikiwithChristine.com also the Facebook site www.facebook.com/BellinghamReikiwithChristine
I also blog at www.asareikimaster.wordpress.com

*FIND A WAY TO COMMUNICATE AND
LISTEN TO YOUR LOVED ONE DAILY. EVEN
IF YOU GET DISCOURAGED, YOUR CHILD
IS LISTENING WHEN YOU SPEAK. THOSE
INTIMATE CONVERSATIONS YOU QUIETLY
HAVE WITH YOUR CHILD ARE HEARD.*

I've always known that life is unfair, I'm sure that everyone finds that out at one time or another along the way. Bad things happen to good people. I know that too. I don't think that losing your baby is either of those things, it goes beyond that.

My husband and I tried for a long time to conceive our first baby, our daughter Ariel. By the time I fell pregnant, my husband Nicholas and I had been together for 10 years and we were so ready for the next part of our journey. So when we found out at our 20-week scan that she was gone, I didn't think it was just unfair or bad luck. I knew it was cruel, plain and simple. Just so cruel.

A social worker came to visit us in the hospital the day after I delivered Ariel. She told me that it will most likely feel like everyone and everything is moving forward around us and we are standing still. She was right, that is exactly what it feels like. Time is working against me because it is passing and giving the illusion of progress, the illusion of healing because it has been a certain number of months since she died. Even though physically I am in the present, my mind and heart live in that hospital room in the maternity ward where I said hello and goodbye to my daughter, all in the same day.

"Everyone goes through tough times," I am told. The words just make me cringe.

"You can have another one," someone else says. But I loved THAT baby, I miss THAT baby, I want to scream.

People talk about me, but they don't talk to me. They pretend not to notice that it is obvious I've spent my lunch break crying in the bathroom. People that have no idea how this feels. People that got to bring a healthy, living baby home from the hospital judge how I grieve for my daughter and how her death has changed me. How dare they? What gives them the right? I wish they would understand that above all else, I am just horribly, terribly sad.

I feel like the only way I could physically show the agony I feel inside is if I peeled all of my skin off. Maybe then, someone would realize. Maybe then they would say, "Wow, you must be in so much pain." But they don't realize, they don't see.

Only you and I know that our babies are just as irreplaceable to us as people's living children are to them. Only we know that we not only mourn for our children but for the life we were promised by their existence. Only we know that grief is really love, and we will grieve for our children as long as we love them, which is the rest of our lives.

I go about my day and work and talk and laugh and do all of the 'normal' people things I'm expected to do, but some days I don't even know why. My daughter is dead, what is the point? What else matters beyond that? I was told that the grief doesn't get smaller but over time the space around the grief gets bigger and more of the good things can get in, the things that bring you joy, the things that make life wonderful. I suppose that's what I'm hanging on for. I'm trudging forward until the space around my grief is big enough and full enough that it feels like I'm really living again.

Dylan Thomas wrote, *"Do not go gentle into that good night. Rage, rage, against the dying of the light."* Even though I miss my daughter more than anything in the world and am terrified of a future without her in it, I'm not ready to give up just yet and for now that has to be enough.

Courtney,

Mother to Ariel

ONLY YOU AND I KNOW THAT OUR BABIES
ARE JUST AS IRREPLACEABLE TO US AS
PEOPLE'S LIVING CHILDREN ARE TO
THEM. ONLY WE KNOW THAT WE NOT ONLY
MOURN FOR OUR CHILDREN BUT FOR
THE LIFE WE WERE PROMISED BY THEIR
EXISTENCE. ONLY WE KNOW THAT GRIEF
IS REALLY LOVE, AND WE WILL GRIEVE
FOR OUR CHILDREN AS LONG AS WE LOVE
THEM, WHICH IS THE REST OF OUR LIVES.

DEAR BEAUTIFUL MOTHER,

I'm so sorry for the loss of your beautiful child. I'm sorry you're here and we have to meet in this way. The loss of a child at any age is devastating. It completely rips a person's insides up. It feels like the world has turned its back on you and that no one understands. On top of all of that, your arms ache and you realize your child is really gone. Your whole life flashes in front of you in just an instant.

How am I going to do this?

Unfortunately, I can't take all your pain away. If I could, I would and I'd bring your baby right back to you. But, if there's one thing I can do, it's let you know what has helped me.

Moments.

In the beginning, I thought I had to take the rest of my life on all at once. The future I had with my son disappeared and there I was, alone and drowning. My anxiety heightened, which made my depression and grief deeper. Every emotion hit me then lingered. I was completely lost.

Life was like this for the first six months (and there are still days I feel like this). It slowed down one morning when I watched the sunrise.

I was able to appreciate the beauty and warmth as different shades of orange painted the sky. It was a crisp October morning and it was like I was the only one awake. The moment the sun peaked felt like a hundred years. I felt my son, Jensen, was in every bird's song and dancing all around me. It was like the sky was telling me to listen and feel what this moment brought.

So, I listened.

The elements soothed me and let me know he was right there with me. This moment also connected me with all the other bereaved moms in the world watching the sunrise. I didn't feel alone and I didn't feel lost.

It also told me…

There are light and dark moments.

There are moments full of love.

There are moments full of pain and agony.

There are moment of support and understanding.

There are moments where everything feels helpless.

No matter the moment you capture, you will power through. This is just one moment and I know you can make it to the next. I did.

Give yourself this moment. Right now.

Take a deep breath.

Feel any emotion you need at this second. Recognize if you're feeling the sadness that pulls you down, the pain that cripples you, or the love that carries you through.

Then, breathe out.

You survived this moment and I promise that I and this tribe of mothers will help you through the ones you don't think will ever end.

We remember your child with you.

We see your motherhood.

We feel the unending love that only a mother has for her child

Always remember, you're never alone in this journey of loss and love.

All my Love and light,

Danielle Ridgway

Forever Jensen's mama

Blog: jensengrey.com

Instagram: @danii_ridgway

Facebook: https://www.facebook.com/MyJensenGrey/

THERE ARE LIGHT AND DARK MOMENTS.

THERE ARE MOMENTS FULL OF LOVE.

THERE ARE MOMENTS FULL OF PAIN AND AGONY.

THERE ARE MOMENT OF SUPPORT AND UNDERSTANDING.

THERE ARE MOMENTS WHERE EVERYTHING FEELS HELPLESS.

NO MATTER THE MOMENT YOU CAPTURE, YOU WILL POWER THROUGH. THIS IS JUST ONE MOMENT AND I KNOW YOU CAN MAKE IT TO THE NEXT. I DID.

DEAR BRAVE, BEAUTIFUL AND BROKEN MAMA,

There are no words that can fix this. I wish that there were, but I've learned that nothing at all can fix this.

There are many words, however, that can help. I hope some of these do.

First and Foremost: You are a Mother.

When my husband, Jonathan, and I lost our first and only child Mathilda, who died shortly before she was born at 40 weeks and 4 days on March 4th, 2016, I needed to hear this. I needed to hear it and read it - again and again and again - before I actually started to believe it.

So, let me repeat that.
You are 100% a mother.

It's hard to reconcile this when your beautiful baby isn't in your aching arms, and your motherhood looks nothing like what you planned. You will still "mother" your child. You will honor them and incorporate them into your life in whatever ways feel right to YOU. Eventually, you may speak their name freely and might even love it when others do the same. To me, there is no sweeter sound than my Mathilda's name, especially when someone else says it. Once I realized that and embraced it, others did the same.

Say what you need.

That is to say, try and communicate as best you can. It's hard. I know it's hard, but the better you get at saying what you need, the better the people who love you can help instead of unintentionally hurting. Tell them what bothers or infuriates you. Tell them how you want them to talk about, or not talk about, your baby. It seems unfair that not only do you have to endure the loss of your baby, but you also have to help people know how to act around you. Trust me, most people want to do and say the right thing. While there is nothing they can say or do to fix this loss, ultimately they will follow your lead.

I have found that it is important to find ways to validate your child's existence and importance in this world. If you want to plan a gathering in their honor - do it. We wrote a service and planned a graveside gathering two months after we lost Tillie and decided to make it an open invitation. So many unexpected people came out to show their love and support and those people are forever sealed in our hearts. If you give people a chance, sometimes they can surprise you.

We have a portion of Mathilda's ashes in a tiny treasure chest. We keep this in her crib and kiss it goodnight, every night. As often as we can, we take her on adventures with us. We both carry her in our hearts, and literally in our necklace urns, but this other physical representation of her, this tiny treasure chest is a way for us to bring her on hikes and bike rides and family visits. Our immediate families know this is our sweet Tillie and they love when we bring her with us. We have started taking photos of the places we go with her, just like any other parents. This works for us and is something wonderful that we can all do together to include her in our lives.

The intensity of your grief is a reflection of the intensity of your love.

The first time I heard this, it really helped me. I was feeling guilty for my emotions and felt like I would never feel positive again. Once I started to think about my pain as a direct reflection of my love, it helped me to not feel as badly about it. The thing is - no one can know the pain you are experiencing. Every writer in this book has experienced the traumatic loss of their child dying and yet, we are all different. We are different people and we experience and cope with these losses in different ways. So while we are all trying to help you feel less alone in this devastating grief (and you are NOT alone), this loss is yours to carry - just like my loss is mine to carry. The weight at first is unbearable, but I have gotten better at carrying it. The event of my daughter dying will never go away and I don't believe that time heals all wounds. Some things cannot be healed. My first child will never physically be here with me and her absence continues to be ever-present in my life. I have found ways to cope that work for me and I promise that you will get better at carrying this loss. It's not a steady climb and it isn't linear, but you will get more used to the weight. Things will never go back to the way they used to be, but you can survive this.

You are irrevocably changed.

You are now a bereaved mother. What a heavy title. The only other word I have come across that gives a name to this new version of myself is Vilomah. It's a Sanskrit word that means 'against natural order - the grey-haired should not bury the black-haired.' I like this word. I wish it didn't have to exist, but I like it. It's not a common word in our culture, but it feels important to have a title after what we've been through, like a widow or an orphan. It validates how different I feel from my former self. As I write this I am fifteen months out from the day my daughter was born still into this world. I am a different woman. Things in my life that used to be important to me are no longer fulfilling. It is hard to recalibrate. It is bewildering to look in the mirror and not recognize the person staring back at me. It has been a really scary time and I am still figuring it out. Everything in your world has come crashing down. Give yourself permission to only pick up the things that help. You will find new things and new people. Some will stay, but you may have to rebuild your life from the ground-up again. Give yourself permission to take your time.

You have been through a major trauma.

Try to be gentle and compassionate with yourself. This is no easy task but it is imperative. Traumatic loss affects you physically, mentally, emotionally and spiritually. Now, more than ever, you need to consider yourself first. So many women are people-pleasers. This is not the time for that. You have to try to let that go and really listen to what you need.

Earlier I suggested that you 'say what you need.' Well, first you have to know what you need and the only way to do that is to be gentle with yourself and listen. It is not natural or fair to outlive your child. Now you find yourself in a world that is over-stimulating and has the audacity to continue on. Everything should stop. No one should get to be happy or be pregnant or have a baby. These are irrational thoughts and feelings, but they might come up for you, they did for me. I had to try really hard not to beat myself up for having these feelings. I had to learn to be kind to myself and put my own needs first. Do not do things just to make other people happy. You are the one in pain. They can be uncomfortable or disappointed if it spares you further suffering after the loss of your beautiful, irreplaceable baby.

Whatever you're feeling is okay.

Try not to feel guilty for your emotions. This is a hard one, I know, but I promise that the better you get at letting yourself feel what you're feeling, the better off you'll be. It's so hard to surrender yourself to the grief and the deep, deep sadness and longing. The anger and blame are intense. I'm sorry that you have to go through it all but, in my experience, there is no running from it. You do have to go through it, one way or another. Try to be good to yourself in the process.

I'm so, so sorry that your child died. It's not only your loss. It's not only your family and friends' loss. It is the world's loss. I like to think that our exquisite babies would have made this world a better place had they lived. I know that they have done just that by having existed at all. Your baby made a difference and will continue to do so in more ways than you can imagine.

Here's to our beautiful babies.
In Hope and Solidarity,

Darcie

Mathilda's Mommy
Born Still on March 4th 2016
www.lostlullabies.weebly.com
https://www.facebook.com/lostlullabies/

THE INTENSITY OF YOUR GRIEF IS A
REFLECTION OF THE INTENSITY OF YOUR
LOVE.

DEAR GRIEVING MOTHERS,

I realized after the death of my son that there was no one word for a mother who has lost a child. We are not a widow or an orphan, as those labels are for other losses. In my case, however, I became a Gold Star Mother (mothers who have lost a son or daughter in service to our country). I also realized that not many people outside of the military had ever heard of the term.

For me, the tragedy of losing my son began on a late summer Sunday night, when the doorbell rang and my husband and I immediately knew that there was something wrong. Mark first opened the door for the two U.S. Army servicemen and he wondered which of our two children brought them to the door. You see, we had both of our sons on active duty with the U.S. Army in Afghanistan at this time. Our hearts were broken and our journey to a "new normal" began with the devastating news that our younger son, Steven had been killed in an ambush earlier that day.

My first motherly instinct was a thought that both boys were alone and far away from family and there was nothing that I could do to help either of them. Scott was informed of the loss of his younger brother while he too was in a fire fight not far from Steven in the mountains of Afghanistan. I have since come to learn that they were both surrounded by soldiers who loved them and these soldiers were family to them in a faraway land. This knowledge that the first tears for Steven were shed by his brothers-in-arms even before I knew of his death has been a great comfort to me. He didn't die alone but was surrounded by others who loved him too.

In the first hours and days after we were informed of Steven's death, my husband took to making phone calls to family and friends and answering the door to visitors and reporters. All I wanted was know the details of what happened to Steven and hear from Scott and embrace them both. In the first few days, I retreated to the privacy of my bedroom and only greeted guests when necessary.

Even though I have a Master's Degree in Counseling, the early days of this tragic time left me often wondering why or even how my husband could socialize so easily. Even when his speech was broken as he tried to hold back tears, he still agreed to interviews and received phone calls from local leaders and reporters. I was often on the verge of anger directed at him when I realized that we both grieve differently.

This was a very important lesson to accept. He needed to speak Steven's name often and tell funny stories about him to anyone who would listen. He needed to be surrounded by people who knew Steven or wished that they knew him. As

I accepted this difference in our grieving process, I was more tolerant and was even able to join him more often.

Mark and I are both active in our local church and our Pastor, Father George and Pastoral Associate, Sr. Mary were such a comfort to me and they were very instrumental in helping me in the early days of this journey to a new normal.

My 9-month old grandson was also a very big comfort to me at this time. His innocence and gentle demeanor allowed me to snuggle him, rock him to sleep, or just watch him play as a way to ease the constant lump in my throat. He provided a brief respite from my sadness whenever he was present. His daddy was on his way home from Afghanistan for the funeral and we were all anxious to have Scott with us and surround him with the love of his family.

I sought out other Gold Star Mothers as a way to feel connected to someone who might understand the pain that I felt. At times, I would be comforted to see a mother who was active and seemed to have her grief under control. Other times, I met mothers who were consumed with the grief and even after many years would still cry at the mention of their child's name. I stumbled a few times but eventually found a way to channel my grief into proudly honoring my son and the ultimate sacrifice that he made. Through various charitable organizations with connections to the military, I was able to share the stories of my son and our short 25 years together.

The lessons that I have learned in the seven years since Steven was killed did not all happen early on in the grieving process or come easily. I am still learning to cope with losing him. However, I have come to know that the loss of a child is impossible to describe or imagine unless you have gone through it yourself. The hole in my heart hasn't gotten smaller with time but instead I have learned to live with it. This new normal has been wonderful with the addition of two more grandchildren since Steven's death but also melancholic knowing that they will never really know their Uncle Steve. I am now able to remember Steven and talk about him without tears even though I will always be sad that he was taken from us too early. I rely on my belief that we will all be reunited one day and I try to enjoy the time with family and friends as much as I can until we are together again.

Sincerely,

Diane DeLuzio

Mother to Steven J. DeLuzio

2/25/85 – 8/22/10
www.sgtstevendeluzio.com

THE LESSONS THAT I HAVE LEARNED IN THE SEVEN YEARS SINCE STEVEN WAS KILLED DID NOT ALL HAPPEN EARLY ON IN THE GRIEVING PROCESS OR COME EASILY. I AM STILL LEARNING TO COPE WITH LOSING HIM. HOWEVER, I HAVE COME TO KNOW THAT THE LOSS OF A CHILD IS IMPOSSIBLE TO DESCRIBE OR IMAGINE UNLESS YOU HAVE GONE THROUGH IT YOURSELF. THE HOLE IN MY HEART HASN'T GOTTEN SMALLER WITH TIME BUT INSTEAD I HAVE LEARNED TO LIVE WITH IT.

DEAR MOTHER,

I know this is a difficult time for you. I've been in your shoes as I, too, am an angel mother to a daughter, Charlotte Joy and a son, Brendan David. I lost them both before I even got to know them, due to miscarriages.

I learned the hard way that there is no guidebook for the loss of a child. Should I use the name I planned for my child or should they remain nameless? What did I do to cause this loss? How do I live my life after this?

I don't have the best answers to these questions, I'll admit. I can only share with you a few things that I have learned over time.

First of all, remember one thing . . . you ARE a mother! Don't let your family, friends, or strangers tell you otherwise. The moment you took a pregnancy test, you received the title of Mother. That will never change!

You may be like me and have lost your child/children before you met them. You may not even know if your child was a boy or girl. My advice to you is go with mother's instinct and name your baby. I lost my daughter at 10+ weeks and my gut told me I had a girl before an ultrasound could confirm it. We named her Charlotte Joy, the name we had planned for her. Naming her was important to my husband and me. Her name said to others that she is real, that she is important, and that she is always our daughter. She and her brother Brendan briefly existed here on earth. They matter.

The third thing I learned is that I didn't cause my children to die, and the same thing goes with you. You protected your child the best you could. There was nothing different you could have done to save your child. Don't obsess over guilt. You did your best like every mother does.

How do I live each day without my child? How do I get out of bed every morning and function? I live each day with the reminder that my children would not want me to stay in bed and cry. They would want me to get up, get dressed and live my life. My goal is to make them proud of me every day. I'm sure they're in Heaven smiling down on me as I get ready for work because I'm succeeding in living another day. I went back to work two years after the loss of my son, Brendan. There are days I want to stay home and cry but I don't give in to it. My children wouldn't want me to be sad all the time or risk losing my job.

Something that helps me survive is that I end my day with a journal for each of my children. I sit down and write them a letter every night. They are told about my day, how I feel and my future plans for tomorrow. Writing them gives me the initiative to get out of bed the next day and do those plans. I feel that I have to accomplish something the next day to make them proud.

So, in conclusion, Mother, remember that your child/children are safe and happy. They would want you to keep going with the life you have been given. Live that life and make them proud of their mother!

Elizabeth

Mother to Charlotte Joy and Brendan David

WE NAMED HER CHARLOTTE JOY, THE NAME WE HAD PLANNED FOR HER. NAMING HER WAS IMPORTANT TO MY HUSBAND AND ME. HER NAME SAID TO OTHERS THAT SHE IS REAL, THAT SHE IS IMPORTANT, AND THAT SHE IS ALWAYS OUR DAUGHTER. SHE AND HER BROTHER BRENDAN BRIEFLY EXISTED HERE ON EARTH. THEY MATTER.

OH, MAMA. I AM SO VERY SORRY.

I am so sorry that your arms are empty and your heart, so filled with love for your precious, irreplaceable child, has been broken and battered with grief.

If you were here with me now, I would wrap my arms around you and simply hold on while you cried the seeming endless tears and wailed for the terrible longing in your soul to be with your child. I would be there, standing or sitting or lying next to you, so that you would know in every moment that you are not alone and that you are loved. I would bring you hot cocoa or tea and warm cookies and listen to you talk about your beloved baby as long as you needed. When you needed a distraction from the heavy weight of grief and longing, I would tell you outrageous silly stories and tug you outside to walk in the sunshine and the trees in a world that, even while it feels it shouldn't, is continuing to move and live.

I desperately wish I could do this with every shattered and grieving mama in the world. Unfortunately, I can't. The next best thing I feel I can do is to write these words and hope that when you find them you will know that you are not alone in this grief and this pain.

I cannot take this pain away from you, not anymore that I could take it away from myself. I cannot really even tell you how you will crawl and fight and live through this unbearable grief that those of us who have lost a child must bear. The journey is different for each of us. But I know that you will. You will bear this most unbearable loss through these dark hours of grief and you will see and feel and experience the light of life again.

When each of my daughters died, it was like the sun was stripped from the sky and all the world was dark and barren. All that I could see was darkness and the heaviness of knowing I would have to live a lifetime without them here with me. I was filled with a screaming rage at the injustice of their deaths and a wailing for the aching longing to hear them, touch them, see them, and hold them in my arms.

I felt more alone than I have ever felt before or after. But I was not alone.

Over time, I found other mothers who have lived and survived this shattering loss. I found people who perhaps didn't understand my experience entirely, but who were willing to stand next to me in love and compassion. With their words and their open hearts and kindness, they reached into the darkness and helped pull me out of that darkness. They brought light into a world gone dark.

And so, with all my love and all my hopes, I offer you these simple words filled with love from my heart to yours. Words that I will repeat over and over until every aching mother like you and like me feels them in her bones:

You are not alone.
You love and you are loved.
And love never dies.

The darkness of grief can never overcome the fierce and abiding mother love that lives in your heart. Love is what will carry all of us through this deepest sorrow.

Always with love,

Emily

Mama always to Grace Hayden and Lily Alise
http://emilyrlong.com
http://facebook.com/InvisibleMothers

*THE DARKNESS OF GRIEF CAN NEVER
OVERCOME THE FIERCE AND ABIDING
MOTHER LOVE THAT LIVES IN YOUR
HEART. LOVE IS WHAT WILL CARRY ALL OF
US THROUGH THIS DEEPEST SORROW.*

LOLA

"You were conceived with love,
You were grown and protected with love,
You were born surrounded with love,
You never had the chance to feel
Anything other than love,
For that I am grateful.

As a mother that has had to say goodbye to her baby I
have learned many things. Such as how life can go from a
wonderful dream to a living nightmare in a heartbeat and
how that moment is forever life changing in a number of
ways.

After having my eldest baby, Beau, 10 months earlier I was
confident and excited about conceiving, growing and caring
for my future babies. Finding out we were pregnant with
Lola was nothing other than a joyful time. I was my usual
confident self, trusting that everything will tick along nicely
and my growing baby would be nothing other than happy,
healthy and strong just like her big brother.

That confidence and our world came crashing down around
us 4 days after our 20 week scan. The midwife phoned to
inform us that our precious baby girl had skeletal deformities
consistent with dwarfism and that we needed to see her asap

to have discussions regarding what we would do next.

An appointment was booked for us to see the maternal fetal medicine team in Wellington for comprehensive scans and tests. Those 10 days were some of the longest days of our lives. The uncertainty was terrifying. We knew so little about what was wrong with our baby and the severity of what we going to face.

My husband and I both came to terms with the fact that our little girl may be exactly that, a small person. But we knew as long as she could have a quality life as a happy, healthy girl we would raise her as we would any other child, surrounded with love and support so she could grow into a strong and confident young lady that could tackle the world head on.

In a small room in Wellington hospital following a very long and nerve racking scan, we waited patiently only to have our world ripped out from under us once again. The words 'Lethal Thanatothrac Skeletal Dysplasia' hit me hard. It was something I had come across in my research, but I had refused to believe that this "death bearing" condition could be something my precious girl would have. But in fact that was exactly what she had. I was in fact living the nightmare I had believed wouldn't happen to me. TD is a form of skeletal dysplasia that causes a bell shape chest alongside many other malformations of the skeleton. Children born with this are usually stillborn or die very soon after birth due to respiratory failure.

We made the hardest decision of our lives, and one that I still think about often, to terminate the pregnancy. The making of this decision was one that was by no means taken lightly. The idea of playing god did not sit well with me but the thought of our baby girl struggling and suffering for her life, if she even made it that far, sat even more uneasily with me.

I gave birth to our precious girl, Lola Gwen, at 22 weeks. The labour and caring for my stillborn baby in the following hours was a whirlpool of emotions. It was the hardest time of my life saying goodbye to the little girl we were only just meeting. I was also overwhelmed by the pride and love I felt for her.

Lola's life, although short, has impacted and helped me in many ways. I have grown to be a stronger person than I ever would have thought possible. She has taught me that nothing in life should be taken for granted. The importance of gratitude, love, and appreciation for everything and everyone, because that has what helped get me through. From this journey I have also learned not to judge other people's decisions as we are all living our own unique journey. We need to make the decision that is right for ourselves. *"A decision made from love is the right one for me."*
Please remember to be kind to yourself and ride this roller-

coaster called grief with love and understanding knowing that there is no protocol or time restrictions. Stay strong and do what needs to be done for you, a loving, wise, and confident mother.

Lots of love,

Emma xoxo

Mother to Lola Gwen

*FROM THIS JOURNEY I HAVE ALSO
LEARNED NOT TO JUDGE OTHER PEOPLE'S
DECISIONS AS WE ARE ALL LIVING OUR
OWN UNIQUE JOURNEY. WE JUST NEED
TO MAKE THE DECISION THAT IS RIGHT
FOR OURSELVES. "A DECISION MADE FROM
LOVE IS THE RIGHT ONE FOR ME."*

DEAR MAMA,

I know your pain is so intense. Maybe you are very new to this journey or maybe this is a road you have been traveling for quite some time. Regardless of the time that has passed since you lost your precious child or the circumstances, the age of your child, or how you're coping at this time, always remember this - your love transcends time and space. It is so strong that no matter what has happened to cause this pain, the love between you and your child remains, brighter and stronger than it ever was. It will continue to grow and evolve. And you, my fellow warrior, you carry the ability to spread the love of your child through this world every day that you live.

There are two thoughts that have been a comfort to me since losing my only child, Matthew. These thoughts are these - each day I live and survive, I am one day closer to spending eternity with him. Regardless of your personal religious beliefs, your child still lives within your heart and science has even recently proven that a mother carries the cells of her child for the rest of her life. Your child still lives.

The other thought that gets me through the hardest times is this - I am still Matthew's mother. We just don't happen to share the same physical space right now. I will always be his mother, just as you will always be the mother to your child.

Nothing can ever change that.

I have devoted my life to honoring my son and his way of living. He was a caring, generous soul. In that spirit, my family and I perform good deeds for others and are in the process of starting a memorial foundation to provide scholarships to his school and the children's hospital in which he received care. It has been rewarding and humbling experience to do for others through my grief. You may find that giving of yourself will help you heal and give you peace.

I leave you with this thought. Life is precious, and now more than ever, please treat yourself with kindness. I know my son would want me to be as happy as I possibly can and your child wants happiness for you also.

You are a warrior. You can do this. I believe in you and so does your beautiful child.

Much love,

Gina

Mother to Matthew, forever 17

YOU ARE A WARRIOR. YOU CAN DO THIS.
I BELIEVE IN YOU AND SO DOES YOUR
BEAUTIFUL CHILD.

DEAR FELLOW MOM OF AN ANGEL BABY,

Take a breath. I promise it's going to be ok even if it feels like it never will be. Although we've never met, I can tell you I can empathize with how you are feeling. Isn't it crazy to think you could love someone so much, even if you've never met them? 5 weeks and 6 days. If you think of that time in terms of a whole lifetime, it doesn't sound so long does it? But that is the length of time it took for me to fall in love with someone that I will never forget.

And in a matter of seconds my angel was gone. Two days before I miscarried, I was driving home from somewhere and burst into tears, feeling like something was wrong. I just knew. Those words resound in my head over and over. I. Just. Knew. When I met my husband, the father of the sweet angel we created...I saw him and just knew. When we saw our dream home for the first time, I just knew. And when those first twinges of pregnancy began to appear . . . I just knew. It was amazing to walk around, holding this magical little secret. I felt so special and so full of purpose. But the day the loss happened, before the ultrasound, before the blood and tears and agony, I just knew.

You are not alone. Just as I was not. Aside from the people that know you and love you, I am here to tell you that it will get easier. The commercials about babies, the announcements from friends that they are expecting, the loss of that little bit of magic in your belly - it will get easier to bear those things.

Here is my advice to you. Raw and unsolicited . . . remind yourself that you are a mom and will forever be a mom. People will give you advice - listen, smile, and forget it. Find a way to memorialize your angel. I lost my angel right before Mother's Day. It was so difficult to see people posting on social media or unsuspecting cashiers wishing me a "Happy Mother's Day." But please, take the time to celebrate yourself on Mother's Day. The second you felt that first twinge or inkling or the moment you read that positive result, you became a mother. Nobody can ever take that away from you.

There is an entire community of women who, when they pray for themselves, pray for all of the other mothers who have lost their angels. Women just like you. Be strong. You've got this.

Gina Longo

Mother to Baby B

*THE SECOND YOU FELT THAT FIRST
TWINGE OR INKLING OR THE MOMENT
YOU READ THAT POSITIVE RESULT, YOU
BECAME A MOTHER. NOBODY CAN EVER
TAKE THAT AWAY FROM YOU.*

DEAR THE BRAVEST OF MOTHERS,

Let me begin by saying I'm sorry. I am so so sorry that you are going through this. I am sorry that you are experiencing a pain that no human should ever have to endure. I am sorry that you are in this "club" that nobody wants to be in. First and foremost, you MUST know that you are NOT alone. I know it feels like you are. I know YOUR world is frozen and time is standing still. You cannot breathe, you're suffocating, and you're numb. It feels like a nightmare, but I'm here to tell you, you WILL get through this, I promise. You walk the streets, stroll through stores, go to work, the sight of happy faces, people laughing, and the sound of children playing stop you in your tracks. I know you're asking, "why me?"

Yes, life does go on, but not yours, not right now. You will eventually get there. No rush, take all the time you need. Scream if you have to, it's okay. Scream as loud as you can. Let it out. Let it all out. You are heart broken, your soul is crushed, and you're completely empty. You will come face to face with family, friends, coworkers and they will say things like, "they're in a better place" or "everything happens for reason." What reason is that? Someone please tell me because I still have not found the answer. Please forgive them, sometimes when they are at a loss for words, these phrases come out. They do not know this suffering unless they experience it for themselves. They mean no harm.

Constant reminders surround us every day - birthday parties, baby showers, friends and family having babies, even a little keychain with your baby's name on it. Until this day, I distance myself from babies, showers, first birthdays, etc., and it's been 7 years. I still have yet to hold a baby since my Vayda. I am too scared that I may lose the feeling of her silky, pellucid yet pure skin.

Grieve how you want, when you want, and where you want, there are no restrictions. Eventually, there will come a time where you will celebrate your baby even if it's just a mention of their name. You will smile and you'll cry and you will still grieve. This is a grief that never fades, my friend, and maybe we don't want it to. You will learn that your grief is the only connection that you have left from your child. I cannot imagine the day that I do not think of my Vayda.

The loss of a child is the loneliest journey you'll ever be on. There will be people and circumstances that arise where people will be afraid to mention your child's name. You may not know this now, but they do not forget. Please forgive them, do not take it personally. We're breathing, we're living, and we're loved. Be gentle, patient, and honest with yourself. You will learn to live again.

As we know such deep sorrow, we also know that beauty of unconditional love. Our love is from a deeper place. Our good days are somebody's mediocre days. Do not let this loss stop you from loving, our hearts can hold so much. Years to come, it will still be difficult to speak of your child, never be afraid to do so. They were here, they were loved, and they existed. I have met so many bereaved parents in the last 7 years and what a relief to share stories. Finally, someone who can relate, because nobody knows your pain and nobody ever will. This is YOUR story.

You will attend one-on-one therapy sessions, group sessions, and even consult with your physician. You may find that nobody can help you. DO NOT give up. Stick with it. You will learn to love again, you'll look at life differently, and your current and future relationships will be different. Yes, I am strong but I am so weak. The love between a bereaved parent and their child is a force to be reckoned with. When you're out with your rainbow child or your child before your loss and someone says, "aww, is he/she your only one?" I'm NOT sorry if I make you uncomfortable with my answer, because no, I have two children, only one living.

Look for signs, you'll find comfort. The day I went to pick up my daughter's ashes, I went alone, I needed to be alone. I come out of the funeral parlor and there was a huge rainbow across the sky. You need to believe in things like this, it's what gets you by. That cardinal on my window sill, "Yup that's my baby."

I am a bereaved mother. I have screamed, I have cried, I struggled to face people, I struggled to talk to people. My whole entire world was shattered. There were times when I couldn't breathe, I literally could not catch my breath. I stopped loving everyone in my path. I became selfish. I'm here, I'm breathing, I love more than ever, I talk to people proudly, and I'm surviving. I am stronger than ever and so are you. This is MY journey and MY story. NOTHING is forever except the love for our children. The depth of our grief measures the strength of our love. We're mothers, our love is unmeasurable. I wish I had the right words to help you at this stage. I wish I could take away your pain. I wish I could fast forward to a place where you will not struggle to get through your days. The only thing I can do is tell you that those days will come, when you're ready. You'll find a place where you will laugh, and a place where you be okay with the mention of your child's name. My favorite quote that I found after I lost my daughter is this:

Butterflies Light Beside Us Like a Sunbeam.

And for a Brief Moment Their Glory and Beauty Belong to our World.

But then They Fly on Again.

And Though We Wish They Could Have Stayed;

We feel so lucky to have seen them at All.
~author unknown

Gloria Netzer

Vayda's mommy

NOTHING IS FOREVER EXCEPT THE LOVE FOR OUR CHILDREN. THE DEPTH OF OUR GRIEF MEASURES THE STRENGTH OF OUR LOVE. WE'RE MOTHERS, OUR LOVE IS UNMEASURABLE.

DEAR BEAUTIFUL MOTHER,

I am so sorry you are here. My heart is broken for you and truly feels your pain.

You do not deserve this.

Right now it may be hard to hear, and it may also sound crazy, but you will be ok. Though, you will not be ok in the traditional sense. You will grow and navigate through this new normal. You will rebuild what you can. There will be a unique beauty in the destruction.

Your baby mattered and they are the beauty in it all. If you never knew your baby past those double pink lines, your baby is beauty. If you never knew your baby after that first ultrasound, your baby is beauty. If you never knew your baby outside of your womb, your baby is beauty. If you never knew your baby beyond those mere moments, hours or days after delivery, your baby is beauty.

Love Always,

Heather

Mother to Hannah Sue Kimble
Website: www.hannahsheartandlove.org

YOU WILL GROW AND NAVIGATE THROUGH THIS NEW NORMAL. YOU WILL REBUILD WHAT YOU CAN. THERE WILL BE A UNIQUE BEAUTY IN THE DESTRUCTION.

DEAREST ANGEL MOMMA

I'm sorry you have had to go through this loss. There's never any real preparation in becoming a mom, let alone a loss momma. No one prepares you for what happens after you leave the hospital. Your heart shattered, your soul filled with a sorrow that can't be explained. How do we live now? How do we simply move on with life with such a huge hole in our hearts? I know this feeling all too well. When I lost my daughter, Madison, many emotions flooded my mind. Why me? What did I do wrong? Why was my body failing her? I will never truly have those answers but I do know I gave my all to keep her safe.

Never really having help for how to cope after we left the hospital, I started to seek comfort in support groups online and met some really great angel mommas close to me. The groups do help but I found the best healing came from journaling. Sharing my day every night in writing to her became a way to stay connected to her. I also decorate her memorial area at home for every holiday.

I wake up every day missing her and thinking she would not want me or her dad to live in sadness. I know she would want us to appreciate life and be advocates to help others like us. To help share that through this long journey without our angels, we can keep living for them and spread awareness to miscarriage and infant loss. I know life may never be the same again, but it can continue.

Life can still have happy moments even in those moments of sadness. Think of your angel and remember the beautiful memories you created with them when they were in your tummy. Think of your angel always being by your side and know that it will be OK. You will survive and grow stronger. All you need is just a little Faith.

Jasmine,

Mother to Madison

LIFE CAN STILL HAVE HAPPY MOMENTS
EVEN IN THOSE MOMENTS OF SADNESS.

DEAR MAMA,

I am a loss mom, like you. I gained this unwanted title just 4 short months ago, when my precious son, Jonah, succumbed to his heart condition and died at 30-weeks gestation. Whatever your story is, whether you lost your precious child through miscarriage, stillbirth, or otherwise, I'm so, so sorry that you and I have to share this title. It's a difficult and heavy one to bear. It will get easier, but it will never leave you.

There are a couple things that I've learned in these first four months since delivering my son, stillborn, into this world. I'm hoping that, by sharing them with you, maybe this letter will help ease your pain just the tiniest bit. Just that one iota of pain relief would be so wonderful for both of us, wouldn't it?

Here goes.

First of all, however you're feeling right now, in this moment, is valid. Your feelings, all gazillion of them at once, are valid. There is no "supposed to" in grief - no timeline, no expectations, no "shouldn'ts" or "shoulds." Whatever place you're at right now in your grief is exactly where you need to be. Feel like crying? Let it out. Feel like a cold, lifeless, feelingless statue while people around you are crying? That happens, and it's okay. Drop all your expectations of grief, and just let it come however it comes.

Next, please seek out supportive voices. You've done that already by picking up this book, so yay! There are more ways, though. Find a grief counselor you like, look for groups online on social media or in forums, or find women around you who've been through loss. It's in these women that you'll find the most comfort and support you've ever had before. We are a supportive tribe of broken yet strong women, and we will hold you up when it feels like you can't.

Third, find what gives you comfort and keep doing it. Through my own experience and through reading what others like to do, I've come up with a handful of things I can do that comfort me, wherever I'm at that day in my grief. At my lowest, it's Netflix or reading in bed. I've also taken a lavender bubble bath almost every day since I came home from the hospital. I write a lot, too - writing letters to your little one is something that a lot of women find comforting, whether it's just scribbled on a piece of paper, in a journal, or on a blog. Try coloring, knitting, reading, doing puzzles, going for walks, adopting an animal - whatever you think might help you feel a little comfort, give it a try. This is self-care, and it's the most important thing you can do for yourself after experiencing such a life-changing, traumatic loss.

Finally, just be kind to yourself. Those words helped me the most after losing Jonah, and they were told to me by other loss moms. These women said "be kind to yourself" and "be gentle with yourself," and I'm so glad I listened to them. The world is a hard place sometimes, and the loss you've experienced is ugly and mean and so profoundly unfair. Treat your body and mind with gentleness and kindness as often as possible. Practice self love.

Finally, love yourself fully and boundlessly, just as you love your baby with every piece of your heart. You are an amazing, beautiful mama. You probably don't feel strong in this moment, but I promise you, you are.

I, and we, are here for you.

Jolissa,

Mother to Jonah Asher Skow
My blog: http://www.letterstojonah.com
My community: http://www.courageousmothers.com

DROP ALL YOUR EXPECTATIONS OF GRIEF AND JUST LET IT COME HOWEVER IT COMES.

DEAR MAMA,

I don't know if this will help. In fact, I know it probably won't. There isn't much that will right now, and for that I am very sorry.

But it's worth a shot, so I've set out to write to you. You've probably heard all sorts of things that people say to you by now. Some may have brought a smidgen of comfort, others may have unintentionally deepened the wound. None of them knew if what they said would help. Nor do I.

I fear that if I divulge the details of my personal experience you will fret over how yours compares. I know I did. Right off the bat, I felt I was insensitive for not being as upset as other loss mothers appeared to be. Months later, that grief I'd suppressed snuck up on me when I least expected it. I then worried that I should be "over it."

I am by nature a competitive person. I want to compare myself to others at all times to see how I stack up. Feelings are not a contest. Yet in my delusion of grief I thought they were. I wanted to "win"- whatever I thought that meant. But there is nothing to win here. Being true to yourself is the single most important thing right now. If you can be your authentic self you are winning, regardless of how it compares to the experiences of others.

So if you want to cry, put on some sad music. If you want to run, lace up your sneakers. If you want to laugh, allow yourself to laugh. And if you're at a loss for laughter now, when it creeps back into your life it will catch you by the most wonderful surprise.

At the expense of sounding cliché, I will leave you with this quote from Mark Twain. *"What is joy without sorrow? What is health without illness? You have to experience each if you are to appreciate the other. There is always going to be suffering. It's how you look at your suffering, how you deal with it, that will define you."*

I hope you deal with your suffering in a way that is most true to your unique self.

Take care and best wishes,

Kae Zaino

THERE IS NOTHING TO WIN HERE. BEING TRUE TO YOURSELF IS THE SINGLE MOST IMPORTANT THING RIGHT NOW. IF YOU CAN BE YOUR AUTHENTIC SELF YOU ARE WINNING, REGARDLESS OF HOW IT COMPARES TO THE EXPERIENCES OF OTHERS.

DEAR BRAVE MOM,

August 25, 2016 was the best day of my life. Our daughter, Hannah Rae, was born. She was born via c-section at 29 weeks but she was healthy, fiesty, and beautiful. She had her momma's eyes, her daddy's nose, and the sweetest little smile we had ever seen.

September 11, 2016 was the worst day of my life and the beginning of the nightmare I relive every day. Hannah had developed necrotizing enterocolitis. She deteriorated rapidly. We tried everything. She was transported to a better hospital where she had emergency surgery. But it was just too late. We had to make the decision and she passed away in our arms at 9:59 pm.

Sweet Momma, I'm so sorry you have to travel this road. It sucks. There's no other way to put it. I miss my girl so much. Please know that you are not alone. Your story is yours and nobody's is the same. But, there are others who walk this awful road and when you meet them they help to keep you standing when all you want to do is fall apart. And sometimes they will fall apart with you. You are not alone, even though it feels like it.

In the early days you will be surrounded by support. As time passes you will find out who your support system is, and it may come from the most unlikely people. There will be people who write letters or send random texts months later. There will be "best friends" who don't come to the funeral. There will be people who push and push for you to "move on." You may have to cut some ties to protect your heart. But you will also make such strong friendships with those who choose to listen and walk with you.

I wish that someone would have told me that there's no right or wrong way to grieve. You just need to do what feels right to you. You may have guilt, I know I do. You may be angry at God or you may run to Him for comfort, maybe both over the course of your journey. You might want to be left alone or you may want company. You may have problems with your partner. There was a span of a few weeks when I thought we would separate for sure. We grieved totally different. He would get frustrated at me for being depressed and getting him "down," and I would get angry at him for making me go out and do things when I just wanted to sleep. Once we were able to talk about it things got better. We were able to understand that we were both reacting differently, but normally to a very abnormal situation. You are doing the best you can and so is your partner. Sometimes it will be hard, but please try to give them grace and ask for grace in return.

Try to find support from those who have walked this road. My infant loss support group has helped me so much. They assure me that I am not crazy for talking to my daughter out loud at the cemetery or for stopping to pick up a white feather or for seeing Hannah in beautiful pink sunsets. They are not afraid to talk about Hannah. We cry, we laugh, we share our babies stories. It doesn't even have to be a support group. It can be an online forum or it can be people you meet along the way who will have coffee with you every once in a while. Just find a support system.

I'm so sorry that you have to read this. None of us should be here. None of this is fair. None of this is ok and it never will be. Just do your best. Keep breathing. Take it second by second. Then minute by minutes. Soon it will be day by day. You are not alone and you are very loved by those of us in this community.

Sincerely,

Kayla Borden

Hannah's Momma
Facebook: Grieve Out Loud
Findinghannahrae.wordpress.com

*JUST DO YOUR BEST. KEEP BREATHING.
TAKE IT SECOND BY SECOND. THEN
MINUTE BY MINUTES. SOON IT WILL BE
DAY BY DAY. YOU ARE NOT ALONE AND YOU
ARE VERY LOVED BY THOSE OF US IN THIS
COMMUNITY.*

DEAR BEAUTIFUL MOTHER,

I wish I had adequate words to express how very sorry I am.
I'm sorry for the unbearable pain you are suffering. I'm sorry
that your world has been shattered into a million pieces.
I'm sorry that you have been forced to endure a splitting
heartache that no one -- no one -- should ever have to
experience.

I know there is pain. So, so much pain. Agony of the very
worst kind. A horrible, empty feeling that won't subside. A
gaping hole in your heart. A nightmare that you can't escape.

I know there will be days, weeks, months where it is a battle
to get out of bed. The hopelessness, the despair can seem
never-ending. It can be draining. I hope you know that it's
okay to be angry. It's okay to be bitter. It's okay to lash out at
God. It's okay to cry. It's okay to wonder why -- why did this
have to happen to you?

But I also know that you are feeling this way because you
love. You have so, so much love for your precious baby. A
love like you have never experienced before. A sense of pride,
tenderness and affection that will never cease. Your child is
beautiful. Your child is perfect. Your child brought you so
much joy while they were with you.

I hope there will be a day when your child's memory brings a smile to your face. One day, I hope you reminisce fondly on the excitement you experienced when you took the positive pregnancy test or the love you felt when you saw your baby moving during the ultrasound. I hope you know it's okay to grin when thinking of your child. I hope you know that it's okay to laugh again. It's okay to feel joy. It's okay to be happy. I hope you know that your ability to smile does not diminish the love you have for your child.

Most importantly, I hope you know that it's okay to talk about your child. To speak of your child's perfection. To share your child's pictures, if you have them. To say your child's name. To write about your child. Keep sharing your child with the world, if you so desire for as long as you desire. And if you prefer to keep your child to yourself, that's okay, too. I hope you know that whatever decision you make is the right one. You are the best mother for your child.

I know that the pain will always be there, buried in your beating, longing heart. But along with that pain is love of the deepest kind. Some days the pain seems too extreme to bear. But when that happens, I hope you think of your love for your child. And I hope you let the love win. Because you a brave mama. You are a strong mama. You are a warrior mama. You are a loving mama. You are a beautiful mama.

Sending you all my love,

Kelly

Loving mother to William Robert Isaacs born on Jan. 5, 2016, and to an angel baby born in May of 2014

I HOPE YOU KNOW IT'S OKAY TO GRIN WHEN THINKING OF YOUR CHILD. I HOPE YOU KNOW THAT IT'S OKAY TO LAUGH AGAIN. IT'S OKAY TO FEEL JOY. IT'S OKAY TO BE HAPPY. I HOPE YOU KNOW THAT YOUR ABILITY TO SMILE DOES NOT DIMINISH THE LOVE YOU HAVE FOR YOUR CHILD.

SWEET MOMMA,

I am so incredibly sorry about the loss of your precious child and for the hurt that your breaking heart is feeling. Please always remember, no matter how long you had with your little one, they will always be your precious baby and you will always be their momma.

My sweet boy, Kiptyn Yase, was born sleeping on Sunday, April 6th, 2014 at 10:19PM. I last heard his heart beat on Friday, April 4th, where the doctor's believed he would be making his appearance before my 40 week follow up and his due date the next week. I had had a perfectly healthy pregnancy after conceiving not only unexpectedly but also miraculously. I had been told I would never conceive naturally due to a diagnosis of Poly Cystic Ovarian Syndrome (PCOS). For nine months, I was able to witness all of the joys of a normal pregnancy. I was overjoyed with every kick, punch, and flip and flop I felt from the inside out. Watching my belly bubble with every hiccup was one of my favorite parts. I just knew I was going to have my hands full. On Saturday, April 5th, I woke up and my very active little boy wasn't moving. My life forever changed at that very moment.

I know how devastating it is to hear that your baby no longer has a heartbeat. I know how it feels to want to do nothing more than crawl into a dark, dark hole. I know how it feels to lie in the hospital bed feeling numb holding your stomach wishing you could bring them back. I know how it feels to know there is another momma across the hall from you who will hold her crying baby. I know that pain…that gut wrenching, unbearable pain. I know how it feels to hear nothing but silence in the room when you delivered your child. I know how it feels to take pictures with your son or daughter who will never grow old. I know how it feels to hold your precious baby in your arms and absorb every second you had to hold them, kiss their cheeks, and let your tears fall on their soft skin. I know how incredibly painful it is to have to hand them back and know that you would never get that moment again. I know what it's like to sit in the funeral home and plan a funeral for your child. No parent should ever have to make the decision whether to bury or cremate their child. I am so sorry.

I know how it felt and sometimes still feels, when someone tells you, "I understand." How could they possibly understand what it feels like? Sweet Momma, there is a community bigger than you realize right now that understands. That community is made of grieving mothers just like yourself whom have experienced the loss of their child. "The Child Loss Community" is what I often call it.

I stumbled across the child loss community one day

while looking for child loss blogs. I came across www.
stillstandingmag.com, where I found blog after blog written
by parents whom had experienced what you and I have. I
remember reading the first one I came across with a tear
stained face, heartbroken for the sweet Momma who had
written the article, and in devastating awe that someone else
knew exactly how I felt. There are articles for holidays, every
day grief, fathers, grandparents, infertility, and many more.
The next blogger I was so very thankful to find was Lexi
Behrndt, writer of www.scribblesandcrumbs.com. She also
has a Facebook page that she posts on often with projects
to do with child loss and her inspirational writings. What
a talented, raw, and beautiful mother. Her words are so
eloquently spoken. Remember Momma, you are never alone.

I am so sorry that all of your hopes and dreams were taken
from you. I am so sorry that you lost the chance to bring
home your newborn to their precious nursery that you
worked on so hard to get ready. I am so sorry that you lost
celebrating their first birthday, the joys of Christmas Day that
is now replaced with pain and dreadfulness. I am so sorry
that your child will not be there on Mother's Day, but Sweet
Momma, you are and will always be their momma. I am so
sorry that you lost the cuddles and the chance to hear your
child tell you that they love you for the first time. I am so
sorry that you will never be able to play dress up with your

little girl and have a tea party with all of her stuffed animals. I am so sorry that you will never get to play in a mud puddle with your little boy and his trucks. I am so sorry that you lost their first day of Kindergarten, going with them on their first drive, their graduation day, and their wedding day. I am so sorry that you didn't lose "just" your baby, but that you lost your future.

My advice for you, Sweet Momma, is this: Don't be afraid to cry, to show your pain, and to let the world know that you lost your child. Don't hold it in. Don't try to be strong for everyone around you. Talk about your precious child and the memories that you have. Hold onto those memories. Lean on your family and your friends. They want to be there for you and they want to help you. It may seem, though, that they're "not doing it right" or "don't know how" to be there for you. They may seem insensitive in the things that they say or they may not say anything at all and that may even upset you more, but just know that their intentions are good. This is a tough situation for everyone. It's okay to let them know you need their comfort but you need them to just sit with you in silence. Let them know you will talk when you're ready.

It's okay to miss your best friend's baby shower. It's okay to hide in the bathroom and cry for the first 15 minutes of your family's Thanksgiving dinner. It's okay to walk out of the store because someone inside asked if you have kids at home that would like the snack they're sampling. I know because I did those things. It's okay to have bad days. It's also okay to have good days.

Start a journal. Write entries with how you feel or write letters to your child. Share these journal entries with others or keep them tucked away somewhere safe. Kiss your precious child's urn every day. Visit their grave. Do something on their birthday in their memory. Keep their memory alive. Find something that reminds you of them and I promise you, one day, you will see signs everywhere. My sign from my sweet boy is hearts. I find them at the most random times, in random places, and it tugs at my heart strings; but it also makes me stop, take a deep breath, and say "Hi baby boy." They're with you. Every single day, with every breath you take, and with every heartbeat, they are with you. Remember, your heartbeat was their safe place and it will forever bond the two of you together.

It's been over three years for me and I find myself missing him more and more with each passing day. I talk about him every day. I look at pictures and wonder who he would be today. I can't promise you that it gets easier. I, personally, haven't found that it does. I still have bad days when I cry and scream into a pillow and ask God why. Sometimes I have the urge to grab that bag of frozen French fries out of the freezer and throw them across the room. But, I also have good days Good days where I imagine him with me, the adventures we would go on and, if I quiet my mind enough, I sometimes think I can hear him laugh. I still have all of his things. I guess one day I will find a way to part with them, or maybe I won't. All I know is right now, I am just simply not ready and that is okay.

Hang in there, Sweet Momma. Take care of yourself and be kind to yourself. Your precious little angel is so proud of you and watches over you every day.

With love and prayers,

Kirsten

Mother to Kiptyn Yase

*THEY'RE WITH YOU. EVERY SINGLE DAY,
WITH EVERY BREATH YOU TAKE, AND WITH
EVERY HEARTBEAT, THEY ARE WITH YOU.
REMEMBER, YOUR HEARTBEAT WAS THEIR
SAFE PLACE AND IT WILL FOREVER BOND
THE TWO OF YOU TOGETHER.*

SWEET MAMA,

Words fall short of adequately expressing how sorry I am that you are here. I wish I had the perfect words to soothe your aching heart. I know that no well-crafted phrase could reverse the devastation or take away the pain that radiates through your core. I wish I could sit and cry with you—sometimes tears speak what words cannot express. My prayer is that my words, and the words of our fellow loss mamas, bring you even just a small bit of comfort as you walk through the unimaginable.

I wish I could tell you that the pain will go away one day. The truth is, there will always be pain this side of heaven. You will always think of your child. You will always miss their sweet face. For as long as you are on this earth, your arms will always ache to hold them. I do not say this to discourage you, but to affirm your grief—it's okay to miss them and to talk about them, no matter how much time has passed. They will always be your baby and you will always be their mother.

Even though the pain does not completely go away, it does change. I know it may seem impossible to imagine right now, but one day your heart will feel lighter. You will smile and even laugh again. Day by day it will get easier to breathe again. Day by day you'll experience more moments of intense joy alongside the moments of pain. I think of it as a series of violent ocean waves. In the beginning, the waves crashed down on my heart daily. Two years later, the waves come less frequently—but when they come, they come with the same intensity as they did in the beginning. I've learned that it's okay to have those days. In a society that constantly tells us to "stay positive," give yourself permission to embrace the hard days. Don't buy the lie that you just need to slap the "band-aid of positivity" on your trauma wound. You have permission to feel, to ache, and to grieve.

I want to assure you that you are not alone. You have a whole tribe of mamas who love you and are here for you. Most people will not understand the pain you are experiencing, but we do. People may become distant or say hurtful things in an attempt to comfort you. Most people care so deeply that they're willing to say anything—even hurtful things—in a futile attempt to help. They usually have good intentions, but simply do not realize that no words could ever take away your pain. It's okay to gently educate them. It's okay to set up boundaries.

I want you to know that it's okay to call yourself their mom. I am a mother to three children—one I had the privilege to hold in my arms for 93 minutes and two tiny babies I never met. Our society often tries to dismiss my motherhood because there are no children in my home, but I know who I am. Yes, our day-to-day lives may be different, but our hearts have been forever changed just like any other mother.

I also want you to know that it's okay to hurt and to question. My faith has always been a foundational part of my life and it was shaken to the core after we lost our firstborn son, Ethan. Ethan was our miracle baby after a three-year struggle with unexplained infertility. When I was 19-weeks pregnant, a routine anatomy scan revealed that Ethan may carry a terminal genetic condition. We begged and pleaded with God for a miracle. Our sweet baby boy was born on August 16, 2015 and lived 93 minutes. I was so angry that God would allow our son to die after so many years of prayerfully waiting. I want you to know that it's okay to be angry and to ask the hard questions. I encourage you bring the hard stuff to God--seek, search, and scream. I was so scared to wrestle with Him, but He drew me close and strengthened my faith as I wrestled. He can handle all of your anger and doubts.

It will get easier to breathe again, Mama. Until then, don't be afraid to reach out and take the hand of someone who understands. We are here with you every step of the way.

Sending you so much love,

Kristin Hernandez

Mother of Ethan Daniel Hernandez and two tiny Hernandez
babies

www.sunlightindecember.com

IN A SOCIETY THAT CONSTANTLY TELLS US TO "STAY POSITIVE," GIVE YOURSELF PERMISSION TO EMBRACE THE HARD DAYS. DON'T BUY THE LIE THAT YOU JUST NEED TO SLAP THE "BAND-AID OF POSITIVITY" ON YOUR TRAUMA WOUND. YOU HAVE PERMISSION TO FEEL, TO ACHE, AND TO GRIEVE.

If you would have told me 10 years ago that I wouldn't be able to have a healthy full-term pregnancy and I would experience a number of losses than one would ever want to admit, I probably would have given you a funny look and told you "It won't happen to me because I'm too young." That was my mindset back then, I always thought the younger you are then your chance of a miscarriage is lower. Statistic wise that is probably true, but I never really quite fit into the statistics of anything.

I became pregnant at a young age, she was definitely unplanned but I would be lying if I said she was unwanted. It has always been my dream to have a big family, I just preferred to wait till I was ready, but life happens. My pregnancy story starts out as your average teenage pregnancy, I guess. Young, with a part-time job at fast food restaurant, and going through it alone. I found out I was pregnant in July of 2012, a week and half after leaving the abusive situation I was in. Yeah, you can imagine the shock when the 50 plus pregnancy tests confirmed my biggest fear. Like I said, she was unplanned and she was by the one person I never wanted to have kids with, but I wanted to keep her. She was not the mistake, he was.

So here I was 21 years old, going to have a baby. Nowadays that's not that uncommon, but few years ago that was frowned upon and I was the talk of the tiny town I lived in. But I wasn't going to let that stop me from being the best mom I could be to my unborn child and give her the life I never got to have as a child.

Days got longer, doctor visits became an every week thing because I have an overactive thyroid and I could never gain the weight to have a completely healthy pregnancy. It was hard, I was alone and I was scared. I had no idea what I was doing or what I was going to do. I remember wishing that I wouldn't be alone in this situation. Fall rolled around, Halloween came and went and before I knew it I was 20 weeks and found out I was having a little girl that I named Alianah Faith. Life was good.

Until two weeks later at exactly 22 weeks when I went into premature labor. By the time I realized it was labor pains and not just your typical pregnancy pains, it was already too late and the doctors could not stop the labor. Her heart was barely beating, but it was there and they were trying to save her. Unfortunately, at 10 am on November 20, 2012, I gave birth to a beautiful sleeping princess. I was devastated and went into a severe state of depression that lasted a year and a half, maybe two years. Time just seemed to stop after my loss.

I finally decided on her 2 year angelversary that enough was enough and I took up the one thing that my life has since been centered around, graphic design. I design artwork and make all kinds of things that focuses on the awareness of pregnancy and infant loss.

I'm not saying that I never break down into screaming or crying fits because I do. I am 26 years old with unexplained infertility because no one can find anything wrong. I get angry and jealous of every pregnant woman I see and every pregnancy announcement seen on Facebook. I have gone so far as deleting every single person who posted an announcement because I can't take it. I won't say that time heals because it would be a lie, but I am saying that time offers better coping mechanisms. I take my anger and jealousy and I make something special and beautiful out of it to give to other mommas who, like me, have nothing to remember their precious babies.

You will scream, cry, and be mad at the world. It doesn't get easier, but I have found that sharing my story, and putting all of my emotions into something productive really helps my grief. At 26 and unable to have kids, my life has completely changed, but I am making the best of an impossible situation and sometimes that's all we can do. <3

Kyla.

Mother to Alianah Faith

I WON'T SAY THAT TIME HEALS BECAUSE IT WOULD BE A LIE, BUT I AM SAYING THAT TIME OFFERS BETTER COPING MECHANISMS. I TAKE MY ANGER AND JEALOUSY AND I MAKE SOMETHING SPECIAL AND BEAUTIFUL OUT OF IT TO GIVE TO OTHER MOMMAS WHO, LIKE ME, HAVE NOTHING TO REMEMBER THEIR PRECIOUS BABIES.

We are the family that didn't get to raise him. If you have experienced a failed adoption you know just what I'm talking about. You are not alone, just as I am not alone. There is an entire sisterhood tribe of us. Even though we prepared our hearts, our home, our finances; we didn't get to bring him into the home that we created for him. He is with another family now. I don't know how he is, or what he looks like or anything about him. My heart breaks over this daily. I write him birthday cards each year for his birthday and I include either money or something special that I want him to have. My hope is that someday I'll get to see him and be able to give them all to him.

I want him to know that no matter what he has been through, we never stopped loving him and we never stopped thinking and caring about him. I love him as much now as the day he came into this world, as much as when we went to court for months trying to bring him home. I hope that I never love him any less, though this is such a hard road. So many people don't understand how I could love him so much. Eli will have three mothers for his lifetime; his birth mother, me, and his adoptive mother. None of us are any less significant than the other. He needs us all.

I belong to a group called *Braving Infertility Together* on Facebook and we also meet in person a couple times a month in different areas. They have been an amazing tribe for me, providing wisdom, caring, support, and a place to fall apart without judgment. There is a global chapter as well if you want to see if they are right for you as well.

The best way to find a tribe is to tell your story to others. Some will receive it warmly and offer support. Others will make placating statements for which you will have dig deep for the grace to forgive them. When you lose a child in this way, not many people from the general public can understand what you are going through. They don't understand that you set up a life for this child - you may have had a baby shower, you baby proofed your house before you were even matched, you were scrutinized about your family history, your health, your house, and your finances. You also went through training, finger printing and more background checks and missed so much work while still trying to hold up those financials that you promised them you make. Most people have never been through that kind of examination before. The special stresses that you went through are not a common experience. My hope is that you find comfort in this book and a tribe of people that you can talk to who are empathetic.

Don't go through this alone. Losing a child in any manner is too much for one person to bear alone. Please reach out to someone, multiple people if you are comfortable, and let help you carry this life-long burden. You are loved, you are strong, and you are worthy. You did nothing to cause this. Some things are beyond our control and it takes time to heal those wounds a little. They may never completely heal, but they will sting less someday. I wish you peace and comfort whenever possible in this journey to your new life, even though it is minus one or more very important people.

Laurie,

A mother to Eli

YOU ARE LOVED, YOU ARE STRONG, AND
YOU ARE WORTHY.

The quality of one's life is not determined by length but by depth. What a person brings to this world while they were here. I proudly say that my son Brian brought so much to so many in the 17 years he was here on earth.

My story began on August 29, 1997, the day I was blessed this beautiful brown haired, blue eyed baby boy. The happiest day of my life. Fast forward 17 years later to November 7, 2014, the day my son was an car accident and did not survive. The day my life as I knew it would be changed, forever.

The day started off like any other morning. I woke up, got ready for work, and woke up Brian for school. Brian came downstairs while I was drinking coffee, all wet in his towel, asking me to iron his clothes for school that day. I, as usual, said "okay." As I was ironing his clothes I had a package sitting on the kitchen counter that was delivered the evening prior. New black boots. I told Brian as I was ironing that he could open the box for me. He opens the box and starts laughing and is like, "Mom, really these are ugly." We are both laughing and I bust out into song and sang "these boots are made for walking and that's just what I'll do and one of these days these boots will walk all over you" and as I'm singing, I'm poking Brian. As he is laughing, he hugs me and says, "I love you." Looking back now at that morning I cherish that hug as it was the last time I would ever hug my son.

The following months I just did not know how I was going to do this. How would I live my life without him? How could this happen to such an amazing young man with his entire life in front of him? He was supposed to be getting ready to graduate high school in June, not be gone. Brian is my life. My purpose. What is life without him?

And then it happened about six months later. . . I laughed. I paused and thought to myself, "How can I be laughing? My son is gone and I'm laughing." I felt guilty. But then I realized my laughing didn't mean I had forgotten he was gone. It didn't make the pain in my heart hurt any less. What it did mean is that I was still alive and that I could miss him and be heartbroken, but yet still experience joy. I know he would not want me to live the remainder of my life in sorrow every single day. I had to accept joy again, just like I had to accept the pain. I had to accept that while I was sad and crying, at the same time it was okay for me to laugh and enjoy life. Not an easy task to do. It is like being on a roller coaster. That's what this journey is like. It took time to accept and truly understand that for me in my life now, sadness and happiness go hand in hand with each other and that's okay. I wasn't betraying my son or his memory by enjoying life. Because of the relationship I have with my son, the opposite would be true. I would be dishonoring him, the bond and love we have if I chose to hide in a dark room and let what is the remainder of my life pass me by. The first day I laughed after Brian's passing was the day I realized there was HOPE.

Here I am, 2 ½ years later living this life without Brian physically here with me. 2 ½ years that I have taken deep breaths and held onto the strength he left behind for me.

There are no easy answers after we lose our child. There are no simple directions to follow. You do not go through the "stages of grief" after you lose a child and miraculously wake up after the last one and be like, "Hooray, I made it, I am healed." This will last a lifetime.

What I can tell you is that I have made it without Brian because I had no other choice but to do so. I made a choice to rise. I made a choice to take the tragedy of his death not have it mean everything. His death shakes me to the core. But his life, oh his life, brings me so much joy. Being his mom is the greatest gift I was ever given. There are so many moments that could never be taken away from me.

I have shed tears each day for 2 ½ years. In the midst of my pain, I have learned to laugh again. I have learned to accept joy. I am continuously learning how to navigate through this world without my son. I fall, a lot. But I always get up.

If someone would have told me that I would still be here after losing Brian in that car accident, I would have told them they were crazy. But I am here. I am living, not just going through the motions each day.

If you are new to this journey of child loss, I am so sorry. My heart aches with you. No parent should lose their child and there are no good reasons, ever, as to why we should learn to live a life without them. But I am here to tell you that you can make it! You can find strength in the weakness. Joy in the pain. Laughter in the tears. You will see this world through a different set of eyes. You will make it!! Never give up Hope! Never give up on the love and bond you share with your child to make it another day! Never let that bond and love die! One day, you will be more than just okay.

Lisa Heath

Brian's Mom

*WHAT I CAN TELL YOU IS THAT I HAVE
MADE IT WITHOUT BRIAN BECAUSE I HAD
NO OTHER CHOICE BUT TO DO SO. I MADE
A CHOICE TO RISE. I MADE A CHOICE TO
TAKE THE TRAGEDY OF HIS DEATH NOT
HAVE IT MEAN EVERYTHING. HIS DEATH
SHAKES ME TO THE CORE. BUT HIS LIFE,
OH HIS LIFE, BRINGS ME SO MUCH JOY.
BEING HIS MOM IS THE GREATEST GIFT I
WAS EVER GIVEN.*

DEAR GRIEVING MAMA,

You may think no one's looking, but I see you. You're lying in a sterile hospital bed, your cheeks streaked with mascara tears, and your stomach deflated beneath a blue hospital gown. Thin sheets cover a womb that is already beginning to shed the remains of a beautiful, much-loved pregnancy. The heart that once beat alongside yours has disappeared, and without it you feel alone and empty.

My heart breaks for you. I see your pain. I see your tears.

Overnight, your hopes and dreams have faded into distant memories. For weeks or months, you've dreamt of downy hair brushing against your cheek and soft rolls of newborn skin snuggled deep against your chest. You've imagined the scent of motherhood: the smell of baby lotion and clean diapers, soft sleepers and fresh milk. You've wondered whether this child would have your eyes, your spouse's smile, your mother-in-law's laugh, or your grandfather's toes. And then all too suddenly, those dreams disappeared and you were left holding nothing but tear-stained tissues and an aching heart.

You are not alone in this. I, too, have been where you are. I have held those fragile dreams in my hands and longed for more. I have said good-bye to four beautiful babies: one buried in a graveyard with an ocean view, the other three buried deep within my heart. I had pictured a home overflowing with the sound of giggles and lullabies, the pattering of toddler feet and the heartaches of teenage drama. And now, no matter how many babies the future holds, our family will always be four short.

I know that this loss has left you feeling weary and weak, drained of energy, and perhaps even exhausted by life itself. You've tried to hide your tears behind tentative smiles and the words, "I'm okay," but inside you're crumbling. Your world has been irrevocably changed. You can't remember the last time you laughed until your belly ached, or what it feels like to cry from pure delight. Real laughter feels like a betrayal to your baby's memory, and you wonder whether grief will always be this difficult. Will your happiness forever be tinged with pain?

Oh, grieving mama, this is not the end for you. It may not feel like it now, but this is just the beginning of your beautiful love story: a love so deep and wide and so all-encompassing, that you will carry it in your heart for the rest of your life.

You will see your baby's smile reflected in the early morning rays, and their laughter will echo throughout the spring wind. Their name will be carried on the tip of your lips, tattooed on your skin, and stretched across countless summer beaches. This little one's life has touched upon yours in a profound, earth shaking sort of way. You will paint, and you will write, you will sing, and you will dance, and all the while, *you will remember.* You may never carry them in your arms, but you will never forget.

You may feel tired and empty but when I look at you, I see nothing but *strength.* It's the sort of strength that comes when one loves in abundance and allows herself to mourn whole-heartedly. It's the type of strength that shatters preconceived notions of what grief *should* look like and simply embraces what it is. It's the strength to get out of bed and face another morning without your baby; the strength to know that tears and pain do not equate to weakness. It's the strength to say, "I am not okay," and know that that in itself *is* okay. Yes, it takes oh-so-much strength to grieve; but you, dear grieving mama, are so-much stronger than you could have ever dreamed.

On the days when your heart falters and your knees feel weak, remember that there is beauty here amidst the sorrow. Remember that this is not the end. While our sweet ones' lives were so much shorter than what we imagined they would be, there is something so beautiful about the fact that we loved and carried them the whole way through. For the entirety of their brief lives, they knew nothing but the warmth and security of their mama. They kicked and swam to the sound of our voices, they dozed to the rhythmic beat of our hearts, and they knew that we were with them.

Still, I know that it is not always easy to find comfort or beauty in such a short life. I know that you still have questions. I know that your heart breaks to see pregnant women around you, and that you wonder why they got to keep what you did not. It seems impossible to find satisfactory answers to the question "Why?" But in our agony, I pray that we may be reminded of the great privilege we were given. No matter the length of time we had with our sweet children, we will always be their mother. In the depths of our pain, we can cling to faith and pray for a peace that surpasses understanding.

And so, dear grieving mama, I mourn with you today. You are not alone in your pain, and you are not alone in your tears. A community of grieving mamas surrounds you, and while we're not a group that anyone joins willingly, we usher you in with open arms and listening ears. We're broken and we're hurting but together we stand strong. Together we will share our stories with tentative voices that grow bolder day by day, and together we remember.

We are here with you. We see your pain and we see your tears, but most of all, we see your strength.

Much love to you,
From One Grieving Mama to Another

Liz Mannegren

Mother to five, one in her arms and four above: Landon, Kära, Björn, and Ebba.

Liz writes and blogs about this journey through grief on her website, www.mommymannegren.com

YOU WILL SEE YOUR BABY'S SMILE REFLECTED IN THE EARLY MORNING RAYS, AND THEIR LAUGHTER WILL ECHO THROUGHOUT THE SPRING WIND. THEIR NAME WILL BE CARRIED ON THE TIP OF YOUR LIPS, TATTOOED ON YOUR SKIN, AND STRETCHED ACROSS COUNTLESS SUMMER BEACHES. THIS LITTLE ONE'S LIFE HAS TOUCHED UPON YOURS IN A PROFOUND, EARTH SHAKING SORT OF WAY. YOU WILL PAINT, AND YOU WILL WRITE, YOU WILL SING, AND YOU WILL DANCE, AND ALL THE WHILE, YOU WILL REMEMBER. YOU MAY NEVER CARRY THEM IN YOUR ARMS, BUT YOU WILL NEVER FORGET.

I am so sorry to hear you have joined this club nobody really wants to be part of.

It's been 6 years and 6 months since we met our precious angel Lilly, when it was hello as well as goodbye.

Even though it's been 6 years I don't think it seems that long ago. To think in August she would be starting Primary 2, that's when it hits me - another milestone we won't get to experience. It's even harder with social media full of it, knowing friends have wee ones starting school and because I work in a school, I can't get away from it. I am happy for them but can't help wondering and imagining what she would have been like. In pictures I see myself and her big brother looking like Lilly. I can imagine her with a personality like her big sister. I imagine she would have blond hair like her brother but with pigtails and ribbons. Wearing a grey pinafore, red t-shirt and a grey cardigan, I imagine her walking up to the school gates holding her big brother's hand.

It's hard to find the words to express my thoughts and feelings on learning to be without Lilly. To be honest it's probably difficult to put in words because I really haven't had to learn. Others who don't understand think I should be over losing our angel. From the outside looking in, many may think I have.

I prefer the statement "still learning to live without Lilly." I really like this because it's more like a process where there is no end and no beginning, there will be lots of things I will need to face, milestones still to come. This shows that every day we will "still be learning to live without Lilly." Still learning to live without Lilly being here doesn't mean she's forgotten, we would never forget her.

She has left such a big imprint on our hearts.

She's on my mind every day, most days not as much, but times like today I think of her a lot. We speak about her always. Her big sister, big brother speak about her, make things in her memory and they often ask what would she be like. Just the other day they were saying she would be starting primary 2 at school. It's hard on us and it's hard for them.

You will never be the same person you were before, you will feel empty and bruised, but unbelievably stronger. You will move through life with understanding and purpose for life so much bigger than you could ever have found without someone leaving your arms.

Just remember you are a survivor, allow yourself time to grieve, to be hurt and angry. Light a candle in their memory, say their name to everybody, look up to the stars. Remember only you can decide the way the rest of your story is written.

I hope in time you find it in your heart to create meaning as this will bring joy in your healing.

Lilly has shown me and taken me on a different journey, it may not be the journey I planned but I have changed as a person. I don't take anything for granted and I make every second count. I am still learning everyday on this journey.

Be kind and gentle.

Love,

Lynsey Berwick

Mother to Lilly Berwick 21-1-11

STILL

STILL MISS YOU

STILL A LITTLE SISTER

STILL A DAUGHTER

STILL OUR CHILD AND ALWAYS WILL BE

STILL IN OUR HEARTS

STILL A WONDER

STILL LOVE YOU ALWAYS

FULL STOP XX

Remember only you can decide the way the rest of your story is written. I hope in time you find it in your heart to create meaning as this will bring joy in your healing.

From one mother of an angel to another,

I know your world has changed forever. I know this can feel like you are living in a nightmare that you will never wake from. I know this is the deepest and strongest pain you have ever known and I am so sorry that you find yourself living this.

I am Megan, mama of angel Kai Phoenix Hajny, who was born silently into the world on the 17th of March 2016. I write this to you over a year after Kai's death and I still can't believe that this story is mine. I write this to you in the hope that this will find some way to reach your heart and help you know you are not alone and that I understand.

There are times I can't even get my head around the fact that I was pregnant, because if I was pregnant then where is my baby? If I had a room prepared for a little someone, then where is he? Did those months happen? My body has found it hard to believe too. It was in such deep shock in the weeks after Kai was born and is only now starting to let go and in some ways get used to having carried and birthed a baby but to be living now without him.

Mama, honestly there were times I didn't think I would survive and other times I didn't want to. I have been to the deepest, darkest parts of me and somehow I am still standing. As bereaved mothers we learn we are stronger than we could ever have imagined. While there are days we feel anything but strong, the love for our babies is the most powerful thing in the world.

Please know you are a mother no matter how long you carried your baby in your body or arms. You are a mother because you will carry your baby in your heart forever.

Right now it may feel like you are drowning in grief. The waves just keep pounding over you and holding you down. It is exhausting and excruciating. As time goes on, somehow there will be bigger breaks between the waves. The waves do come, I guess they always will but they do come less frequently so you can find your breath again.

Please know you are not alone and that sometimes it will feel like there is no hope. Some times it may feel like you will never know lightness and joy again, but from one who has been there, those moments will come over time. When they do, please know this is ok. It is ok to find happiness again. It is ok to look forward to the future. You will always love your baby. You will remember them forever.

Sweet mama, be loving and be gentle on yourself. You are now living a life that no one but another grieving mother can understand. While this can feel lonely, there are so many who want to support you and care for you, so please let them. You need and deserve to be nurtured and cared for like any new mother.

This is not the motherhood you imagined. This is not the childhood you dreamed of for your baby AND this is your precious life in all its imperfection. You will learn how to be the best mum you can be to your dear angel baby. Your parenting will look different but it is still so important. You are a mother!!!

From my grieving heart to yours, I send you so much love. I honour your precious baby and mothering heart.

May you find peace,

Megan

Mother to Kai Phoenix Hajny
Earth Mamas of Angel Babies Facebook Group
https://www.facebook.com/groups/1736383746607802/
Some memorial handmade heArtworks
https://www.etsy.com/uk/people/AtiyaCreations

Inner World Village- supporting women after their world has changed forever, to heal and in turn help heal our planethttp://www.innerworldvillage.com.au/

SWEET MAMA, BE LOVING AND BE GENTLE ON YOURSELF. YOU NEED AND DESERVE TO BE NURTURED AND CARED FOR LIKE ANY NEW MOTHER.

DEAR BEAUTIFUL MAMA,

I want to tell you some things that I wish I would have been told when I first found out our beautiful first born son, Lachlan Michael Eagle Mueller, had died in my womb at 33 weeks. You did nothing wrong. You did everything right and unfortunately it was all stolen from you and your beautiful child. There are going to be people who say very hurtful things or want you to get over this agonizing loss and because they have never been here they have no idea and their opinion doesn't matter. You will never get over your child dying. You will live everyday with the "*what ifs*" no matter how hard you try. One day the tears will stop flowing as often but your heart will never stop hurting because you are missing an integral piece of your being. Any child dying is out of the natural order of life and it should not happen but it does. I learned very early on that it happens way more than I ever could have imagined.

The child loss community, this collection of mamas will surround you and they will love you. They will show you that everything you are feeling and doing for your child is completely normal when no one else understands. One big thing is no matter how many people surrounded me early on, I still felt alone - like the quicksand was going to swallow me whole and no one else would be able to help. This community has shown me so many times that I am not alone. When I was having thoughts that I thought were insane, I would see someone post exactly how I was feeling and know others were there to (although it unfortunate anyone else has to walk this journey, you are NEVER alone).

I have always explained the grief from Lachlan's death as an ocean. In the beginning the waves were so strong I wasn't sure I would ever be able to get my head above water, it seemed like I would take a little breath and then another wave would pull me right back under. As the months went on there was a time where I could get a little bit of calm in that ocean, it was still rocking but my head was a little more above the edges and I could start breathing again. It takes time but I promise that there is some breathing that will take place without the waves crushing you so frequently. There are still days where it feels like that ocean is taking me under tow and I just can't get out but then somehow, someway there is a calm.

The crazy thing is that to the outside world, nothing has changed. I mean, yes, they know that we lost our child but because most people did not get to meet our son, as we live very far from our family and friends, it was like he never existed to them. We were still just the two of us living life but it's so different. We can't be those same two people we were before Lachlan died because that just isn't life. We had planned the next year of our life with our son (let's be real, the rest of our life) and now we were just the two of us again. We had his nursery set up for our baby boy that never got to even see or be in it and built a house for a child that we didn't get to keep. You will never be the person you were before this tragedy struck your life. It is just impossible to be the same person when everything that you hoped, dreamed, and were living for has changed so drastically.

People will treat you different from the way they did before. I don't know how to explain this in a way that makes sense, but it is almost like they treated me like I was made of porcelain and if they talked to me like the human being I was, then I would break. It makes me angry because there are still people who do it. We lost a lot of the friends in our life that we thought would be there for us. Your child dying really puts it into perspective who your true friends are. You will see people you haven't talked to in years come out of the woodwork and be the best people that you may not have even realized you had in your life. Unfortunately, you will also see some of the people you thought were your best friends become no more than acquaintances (if that) who you don't even want to talk to or be around for that matter. I can tell you from my stand point you are better off without those people because those who can't stick around at the hardest of times, should not get to be there for the best of times. People seem to be perfect when things are going great but when they cannot be decent human beings when life gets hard, it's a cop out.

Please know that there will be triggers and there will be many of them. You will not know in the beginning what they are or when they will happen but they will. I had been very good at putting on a face when it came to grief in the past but when it's your child I feel like there is just no control, no certainty on when you are just going to lose it. I knew for a fact that I could not be around newborn baby boys in the beginning, but what I didn't know was that when I came back to work I would see a child with Lachlan's day of birth (April 1, 2016) and burst into tears before I even had a chance to comprehend what was happening. There were lots of these times where I would just breakdown and I could not stop myself. Be gentle with yourself because it feels impossible and it's not going to be easy by any stretch of the imagination.

Again, you need to tell yourself that this is not your fault. I struggled for a long time with not being able to believe this and there are still times, even after 14 months, that my head goes back there. Deep in my heart, I know I did my best; that he was healthy and perfect, that I had no control over the disaster that became my life. The unconditional love you feel for your child will only get greater as the days goes by and there will always be a hole in your heart the size and shape of your child. The Lachlan sized hole in our hearts will never go away, it is something that we are learning every day to live with. We include him in our day to day life just like anyone else does with their living child. He is a piece of us and we will continue to shout his name from the rooftops for the rest of our lives because he is ours and we are his. I hope that you do the same for your child, you may feel that it is hard to talk about, especially in the beginning and you can make whatever choice feels best for you. I promise you that hearing their name, saying it out loud and allowing others to use it will help your beautiful mother heart. Be gentle on yourself and practice self-care as much as you can. You are an amazing mother to your baby who only ever felt your unending love.

Sending you so much love and light,

Melissa

Lachlan's mommy forever and always <3
Lachlan Michael Eagle Mueller born still on April 1, 2016.
Our first and forever little love.
(blog: www.wordpress.com/lachlanslove)

YOU DID NOTHING WRONG. YOU DID EVERYTHING RIGHT. THIS WAS NOT YOUR FAULT.

DEAR SWEET, BRAVE, STRONG MAMA –

I know your heart is broken. Shattered. Obliterated. I also know that you may not feel (or want to have to be) strong or brave, or anything remotely close to those descriptors. But you are. And one day, you'll look in the mirror, straighten your back, level your shoulders, raise up your chin, look yourself straight in the eye, and know, deep-down, that you are a survivor. That you have done - and will continue to do -hard things. The hardest of things. And it's all because of love.

Love. You grieve so deeply because a deep and abiding love existed first. You will love your child just as much, just as unconditionally, in death as you would have in life. There are seemingly endless differences between parenting a living child and parenting a child that has gone beyond our reach, but that is not one of them. Love will endure, long after we are gone, and I believe it can reach our children, wherever they are – far beyond the moon, and the stars.

This life is far from fair. And I'm so truly sorry. So many bereaved moms I've connected with have expressed their innate desire to turn back time -- to relive the precious moments of their pregnancies or the all-too brief time they spent with their child/ren outside of the womb, because there is just never, ever enough time -- or perhaps to have the chance to do something, anything, differently, or make another choice that could have maybe, just maybe, resulted in a different outcome. Something that would make this nightmare just that: a bad dream that we'll eventually wake up from. But we can't. Our reality is horrifying and it is exhaustive work to get through each day. Putting one foot in front of the other despite such intense pain and hopelessness is, at times, excruciating. All you can do is take life one day at a time. And at first, one day may seem too daunting so you start by taking it one moment at a time; until those moments can be strung together to make an hour, then a few hours, then a day and so on, one foot in front of the other.

I wish I could rewrite your story. I wish I could rewrite *all* of our stories. I wish I could reach through these pages and wrap my arms around you. I wish I could sit beside you and hold your hand. Because I so desperately want you to know that you are not alone. Despite how it may feel, you are not alone. We are out there, grieving right alongside you, for our own children as well as for the children of our fellow loss mamas who share our sorrow and pain. Who feel as lost and as hopeless and as gutted as you do, right in this moment. Your suffering is not foreign to us and we do not shy away from it. We see you. You are not alone.

I hope you know that you are loved and beloved. That your

child is loved and beloved. That their life matters, and that it made – and will continue to make – an impact. Unbelievably, in time, the grief will find a way to co-exist with any future joy you find still exists for you. I know it feels impossible, but there is joy waiting for you, right around unforeseen corners. It may not look like it once did (and I know how unfair and troubling that is) but you will smile again. You will laugh and feel something besides rage or pain or brokenness. It will take time, likely a long time, but it will happen. And, you may feel guilty for smiling or laughing or feeling joy but you are human. There is no roadmap for living life post-loss. There is only empathy and time and love and compassion. Hold on to those things whenever and however you can, for they are your lifeline. Find your people and hold on tight. They are the ones who will help ensure that your child is never forgotten, and who will keep their memory tucked carefully and lovingly into the folds of their hearts, forever.

There are so many, many layers to our grief and the lifelong road to healing is complicated and messy. But we just keep taking it one day, one step, at a time and I hope you can find even the smallest bit of comfort in knowing that even though our stories differ, the sorrow and pain and devastation we carry with us every day is understood by each of us who find ourselves walking this path. Ours is a unique sisterhood, a bond that cannot be broken. You are not alone.

Wishing you peace, comfort and love -

Melissa N.

Mama to our little bird, Evelyn Amanda

*I HOPE YOU KNOW THAT YOU ARE LOVED
AND BELOVED. THAT YOUR CHILD IS
LOVED AND BELOVED. THAT THEIR LIFE
MATTERS AND THAT IT MADE – AND
WILL CONTINUE TO MAKE – AN IMPACT.
UNBELIEVABLY, IN TIME, THE GRIEF
WILL FIND A WAY TO CO-EXIST WITH ANY
FUTURE JOY YOU FIND STILL EXISTS FOR
YOU.*

Dear Mama,

I'm so sorry you're here. This is (as many have surely said) the club no one wants entry to. There's a darkness around you now, I know. An emptiness and a fear of the future, both immediate and long-term. And so, so much time.

One of the hardest parts in this loss is time. It's hard to see anything in the midst of the trial, yet everything feels as if it is moving in slow motion. It's the paradox of having all the time in the world and having nothing to do with it.

If I can offer one piece of advice for this moment it is to simply allow yourself to feel. Give yourself over to every emotion that comes through you and let it out. It is the one true benefit of this otherwise painful span.

Sometime after you've broken over and over again, a second timespan will arise. This new period will bring a small crack in the clouds and take you from an endless expanse of sorrow to a time of finding peace. This is when you look for the signs that your angel hasn't left you. It's when you put your heart in touch with remembering every special moment of their life instead of reliving the pain of their death.

This is the time that allows you to establish your child's legacy. Don't be afraid of feeling sad at this point or shedding tears, though. As with any great love, there is great sorrow when they're gone.

Just remember to continue to seek the light through the darkness. However the light comes to you (a perfect rainbow, a touching song, a particularly beautiful sunrise), embrace it and let it into your soul. This is the time your angel has given you. Lose yourself in it and the joy of drawing close to them.

Pamela

Mother to Nathaniel Leon Homolka; Mia Opal Elena Homolka; and Lucas Iain Homolka.

JUST REMEMBER TO CONTINUE TO SEEK THE LIGHT THROUGH THE DARKNESS. HOWEVER THE LIGHT COMES TO YOU (A PERFECT RAINBOW, A TOUCHING SONG, A PARTICULARLY BEAUTIFUL SUNRISE), EMBRACE IT AND LET IT INTO YOUR SOUL. THIS IS THE TIME YOUR ANGEL HAS GIVEN YOU. LOSE YOURSELF IN IT AND THE JOY OF DRAWING CLOSE TO THEM.

DEAR BEAUTIFUL MOTHER,

I know.

I know how it feels to have your heart feel both heavy and hollow.

I know how it feels for your arms to ache from the emptiness they are holding.

I know that your life will never be the same. There is no going back to the way things were.

I know how it feels to wonder if life is still worth living.

I know the thudding realization that hits you, square in the chest, the moment you awaken. The one that reminds you, "My baby is gone."

I know how it feels to be surrounded by people you don't want to see because the one person that matters most can't be here.

I know how the guilt feels. You've done nothing wrong, but the guilt has this terrible way of invading your mind and trying to convince you otherwise.

I know that the sight of other people being happy with their children makes you wants to scream and throw things.

I know how it feels to look in the mirror and not even recognize the person staring back at you.

I know the feeling of watching your dreams shatter and knowing you will never be able to put the pieces back together in the same way.

I know that you love your baby with every ounce of your being and I know that love will never go away.

I know that you're exhausted. You will always be exhausted. Grief is exhausting.

I know that words will do nothing to change what happened. But, I also know that words have power and they can provide shelter in a time of need.

I know that you don't want to be reading this letter. I wish I wasn't writing it.

Finally, I know that you are loved and that you are never alone in this.

Love,

Rachel

Mother of Dorothy

2/22/16

https://anunexpectedfamilyouting.wordpress.com/

I KNOW THAT YOU ARE LOVED AND THAT YOU ARE NEVER ALONE IN THIS.

Dear Beautiful and Fragile Mama,

I wish I could take away your pain. You know the pain where you feel like you are on a never ending emotional rollercoaster and you feel like you can't breathe, think, speak or go on. You have been forced to deal with the fact that your baby is gone and you are still here. You would do anything to take their place. This curveball that life has thrown at you will change you, but it doesn't have to destroy you.

I, too, have experienced this. I, too, know the excruciating agony that comes with losing a child.

Losing a child that you tried for and wanted is devastating. Losing a child makes you feel like your heart is shattered into a million pieces.

You doubt your self-worth, you blame yourself, and you might even begin to hate your body. You, unfortunately, may have come to realize that emotional pain hurts so much more than any physical pain could. You will always love and miss your child and you will never forget them, no matter how heartbreaking it is to remember them.

I wish I could tell you it will get easier, that the grief will lessen over time. But the hard truth is that your grief will come in waves. One day, you will feel like you are finally getting your feet back on the ground and the next you will feel like curling up in a ball because you are reliving every bit of pain and sorrow from the day your world came crashing down.

What I can tell you is that you will carry on. You will survive and there will even be days where you smile and laugh again. That is okay.

It's not a matter of forgetting about what happened, but realizing you're so much more than what has happened. You'll look at the world through a totally different lens. Your loss will change you in many ways.

So, please, sweet fragile mama, choose to live for that baby.

Choose to take, not only the sadness and the heartache, but also the memory of your precious baby and use it for something positive. Choose to go on living, choose to be happy, hopeful and to find joy. Choose to be someone who opens their heart up to carry another bereaved through this difficult journey, the journey where you need someone who truly understands what you are experiencing.

Most importantly I want you to know that you are not alone. I am with you and so are all the other bereaved moms. I am here as a testament that you will make it through this time in your life. Even though it may not feel like it now, you will get through this. You're part of this community now. It's not a community any woman sets out to join. But it's a community filled with other warriors just like you - women who have had to say goodbye to their babies before they even had the chance to say hello.

Randi Schlenker.

Mommy of Journey Schlenker- Too Beautiful for Earth

WHAT I CAN TELL YOU IS THAT YOU WILL CARRY ON. YOU WILL SURVIVE AND THERE WILL EVEN BE DAYS WHERE YOU SMILE AND LAUGH AGAIN. THAT IS OKAY. IT'S NOT A MATTER OF FORGETTING ABOUT WHAT HAPPENED, BUT REALIZING YOU'RE SO MUCH MORE THAN WHAT HAS HAPPENED.

DEAR MAMA,

If there is one thing I want to tell you, it is just to "hold on".

You are on a journey that is likely to last the rest of your life, a journey you did not choose or expect for yourself. At the beginning the pathway is incredibly bumpy and you lose your way all the time, but just remember to hold on. After a few months the path ahead may become a little clearer, but it will still be bumpy. A few more months on and the bumps will be fewer, you may lose your way from time to time, but keep holding on and the path will be easier to follow.

I lost my only child, James, nearly 18 months ago, and this is where I am. The path is still bumpy at times but compared to the start it is smoother now. I didn't know how I would ever get this far on my journey. It has been the hardest journey of my life, but I have held on, even on days where I didn't think I could take it much more.

Don't try to rush the journey. There is no easy way through it. As hard as it is, just hold on and you will travel further along. There are so many people who know how hard it is for you as we have been there too.

At times you will need to hold on to every last bit of hope you possess. Negativity can creep in, and it can be hard to be positive. On good days try to look for some positives, perhaps about your child. They were a blessing and a beautiful gift, and even though they cannot be here in your arms, please believe that there WILL be brighter days ahead and there is more to look forward to. It may not seem like it at times, but the storm will eventually settle and you will create your own path.

Try to find people who can help you through your journey, be they your partner, a relative, friend, others in the baby loss community, a therapist or counsellor. Talk to them about your feelings. You can't embark on this journey all by yourself or it will be even harder and take longer to navigate. You need someone to care for you and will you on when you feel you don't know how to continue.

Hold on to the beautiful memory of the feelings you had with your child to help you through the rough times, and don't ever worry that you will forget your baby. I still love James as fiercely as the day he was born, and he will always be one of the most important things that ever happened to me. How could I ever forget him? We don't know what life has in store for us, but I know that my beautiful James will be with me throughout the rest of my life, in my heart and my thoughts, and I won't move on without him.

Hold on to the love you have for your precious baby. This can help you stay on your path. Capture this love as you embark on your journey by writing letters or poems to your baby, creating drawings, collecting things that remind you of them – do anything you think of that will help you to form a lasting connection with them, allowing you to express your emotions. Through the dark times this focus can help you to hold on.

Lastly, hold on to the thought that your baby would have loved you, as much as you love them. You would be the most important person in their life and they would have only wanted good things for you too. Try to remember this as you go down your path.

Hold on to the love, not the loss.

Rebecca

Mother to James

My blog is https://littlenutbrownhareblog.wordpress.com/

HOLD ON TO THE LOVE, NOT THE LOSS.

DEAR MAMA,

There is so much that I can say to start this but let's just start it with *this sucks.*

This absolutely sucks because if you've gotten this book, chances are you've lost your baby.

Now more than ever you'll realize that words you thought were comforting for others who lost loved ones anger you. You may not want your child to be called an angel, you may not want your subsequent children to be called a rainbow baby... and that's okay. To each their own – this is something that is highly important.

But, even more so, remember that we all grieve differently. My grief is not your grief. Your grief isn't mine. All I can offer you is some advice on what has helped me and hope that it may help you or may point you in a direction that may help.

To me grief is walking on the edge of the ocean and as you're walking the waves are hitting your feet. You keep walking, and all of a sudden a riptide takes you in. You're fighting against the waves and struggling until you finally break away – and you continue to walk along the ocean ...

It's been 5 years since I lost my son. In those 5 years, I've learned so much. It's **okay** to smile. It's **okay** to laugh. Just because I do these things doesn't mean that I miss my son any less. Even now, I can be doing well and then a trigger comes up and I'm fighting against that riptide to come back up for air. I wish I could tell you that it gets easier or that it gets better but it doesn't. It just gets different and you learn to live your life for your baby. That's what I do. Every new experience is an experience that he never got – but an experience that he did "get" because he's with me – *always*.

Here are some things that have helped me in my grief:

Traveling – anywhere, even if it's just a day trip. Experiencing something new is so important in my grief journey and has really been a cornerstone in helping me cope.

Positive affirmations – thank you, Pinterest. I constantly look for positive affirmations to "boost my mood." Sometimes it works, sometimes it doesn't.

Gemstones– How I love a good gemstone either wearing it or having it in my hand – the comfort a "rock" can bring.

Water – when traveling if I can be near water, I will be extremely happy. Whether it's a creek, waterfall, ocean, lake or pond, watching the water and seeing the wildlife that comes near it is just serene.

These are just some of the things that bring me joy. I truly hope that you are able to find something healthy that brings you joy and enjoy it to the best of your ability. Keep experimenting with what makes you happy because you may find new hobbies that you never realized were of interest to you. I like to think of this as our children giving us a part of who they would have been had they grown up.

Don't be discouraged if your friendships change because that's what happens – some people just don't know how to grieve with us. They don't understand how we could miss our child so much. Mostly because they've never experienced it. Your friends don't always know what to say, but the right friend will fight against everything to prove that they are there for you. You may find support with other moms who have lost a child as well. It's important to remember that just because you both share that common bond, it doesn't necessarily mean that you need to be their friend or even their friend later on. Make sure that your personalities fit well together because friendship is so important.

Lastly, always remember to be gentle with yourself. It's completely normal to feel like you've taken steps back. But you know what? You're trying and that's all that really matters.

Sending love and hope to you xoxoxo

Shannon

Cameron's Mom

I TRULY HOPE THAT YOU ARE ABLE TO FIND SOMETHING HEALTHY THAT BRINGS YOU JOY AND ENJOY IT TO THE BEST OF YOUR ABILITY. KEEP EXPERIMENTING WITH WHAT MAKES YOU HAPPY BECAUSE YOU MAY FIND NEW HOBBIES THAT YOU NEVER REALIZED WERE OF INTEREST TO YOU. I LIKE TO THINK OF THIS AS OUR CHILDREN GIVING US A PART OF WHO THEY WOULD HAVE BEEN HAD THEY GROWN UP.

This would normally be the time that someone welcomed you to the club you've joined. But let's face it...there is nothing normal about this club, and you definitely didn't ask to join it.

None of us did.

Regardless, we are very welcoming. Your race, religion, sexual orientation, political alliances . . . none of that matters here, because you're one of us now, and we all need to stick together.

Since you're here, I want to tell you a few things I've learned...

It's okay.

Not this situation. This situation sucks.

But everything else? It's okay.

It's okay to cry.

It's okay to not.

It's okay to be sad, upset, or angry.

It's okay to quietly accept what's happened, and it's okay to be pissed off at the entire world.

It's okay to blame God, the universe, fate, or whatever . . . but please don't blame yourself.

It's okay to have bad days.

It's okay to stay in bed for a week.

It's okay to carry on like nothing happened.

And please, remember that when you're ready, it's okay to be happy again.

It might take a while, and you might need some help getting there, but I really hope you do.

I also want to share something important that an amazing woman, Gran, told me when I joined this club...

You are a mother.

You created that child.

You carried them as long as you could.

You wanted them, and you loved them their entire existence.

You ARE a mother.

No one can EVER take that away from you, and don't you dare let anyone tell you otherwise.

Gran was a smart woman.

I am a mother.

So are you.

Nothing can change that or take it away and I can think of no one more deserving of the title.

Tamaira De Vries-Liverance

(@Infertile_Nanny)

Angel mama of 2

Both born far too early on June 22nd, 2014 & November 19th, 2014

YOU ARE A MOTHER.

YOU CREATED THAT CHILD.

YOU CARRIED THEM AS LONG AS YOU COULD.

YOU WANTED THEM, AND YOU LOVED THEM THEIR ENTIRE EXISTENCE.

YOU ARE A MOTHER.

NO ONE CAN EVER TAKE THAT AWAY FROM YOU AND DON'T YOU DARE LET ANYONE TELL YOU OTHERWISE.

HI MUMMA,

So, I could tell you it gets easier, because I know that's what I wanted to hear too. By now I've worked out that my recollection of the experience is just as raw as if it were playing out again. An endless repeat. The moment I held my daughter in my arms and kissed her still body. Scratch, the needle goes back to the start to play your song again.

Those moments never change, you will always recall them, and you know what, don't ever be afraid to. For me those moments are a strongest connection to my darling daughter. Yes, they are painful. Yes, they make me cry but we are always together in my memory, as mother and daughter. The saddest song we could ever write together.

It's those memories, with all their pain and sorrow that actually contain some of the truest love. As time goes on, what I see now is that when I recall those memories I have to make a conscious effort to bring forward the immense love I felt in those precious moments together. I don't push away the sorrow, how can you when it wells up enough to cry an ocean, but I make room for the love to shine.

Don't be afraid of your tears or try to force them to stop. You cry because you loved. You cry because you lost something you loved so very deeply that, at the time, it would seem your heart could never be whole again.

I know now that I don't need my heart to be whole again. My daughter, when she died, took part of it with her and I am happy for her to have it. It is what connects us, it is what keeps her memory safe - my love for her and the piece of my heart she carries with her everywhere. The unbroken golden chain that connects us as mother and child, in life and in death. She is my child. We sing our song together again.

And your child too. I know you won't ever forget the circumstances of your loss, and I beg you not to. We never asked to be bereaved parents - who would? But it's a part of who we now are.

Move forward in your life. You have to, otherwise it will move on without you and that's when you stagnant in your grief, fixated on guilt and blame. Don't feel ashamed - we all do it – feel that deep sense of guilt only a parent who has held their dead child can feel. The blame, ohh the blame! We blame ourselves constantly. What did we do wrong? What did we do to deserve this outcome? Well, you didn't deserve that tragic outcome, but trauma doesn't discriminate, it's unpredictable like that. I'm so sorry you had to go through this too. We are all still in shock.

Remember the unique connection that is between you and your child, it is still there, it is always there. It will be hard to see sometimes because of the tears, the anger, the frustration, the blame, the depression, the anxiety, the fear.

Let those feeling come and go, but always hold onto the love, the unbroken bond you created with your love. It is always there - recall it, love it, embrace it and hold onto it, because the love is what connects you. The invisible golden thread of two hearts that loved. The song only you two can sing.

From my heart to yours,

Jill Heike-Woods Xx

Mother to Claudia Marie Woods
Website etc: www.thestilllifeproject.org
and the FB group: The Still Life Project

*DON'T BE AFRAID OF YOUR TEARS OR
TRY TO FORCE THEM TO STOP. YOU CRY
BECAUSE YOU LOVED, YOU CRY BECAUSE
YOU LOST SOMETHING YOU LOVED SO VERY
DEEPLY THAT, AT THE TIME, IT WOULD
SEEM YOUR HEART COULD NEVER BE
WHOLE AGAIN. I KNOW NOW THAT I DON'T
NEED MY HEART TO BE WHOLE AGAIN. MY
DAUGHTER, WHEN SHE DIED, TOOK PART
OF IT WITH HER AND I AM HAPPY FOR HER
TO HAVE IT.*

DEAR MAMA,

Words cannot begin to describe the pain you are going through. Yet, words from people who don't understand can worsen the pain.

I know you never imagined you would be in this situation, I know I never did. You'll have days where your grief is manageable, but out of nowhere you'll have days where you don't feel like getting out of bed. Grief is now part of your life and it will be until your last breath, make friends with it and accept that grief is a part of your life.

I'm three years out from my first lost and two years out from my second loss - time doesn't make the loss any easier. Remembering your baby(ies) is what will help with your loss. We include them in what we can. We visit our daughter's grave on the holidays and on her angelversary, we take flowers and spend time sitting at her grave.

Do whatever helps you cope. If that means taking a break from social gatherings like baby showers, do it. Now is the time to care for your broken heart and do what won't make your loss any harder. Take care of you and your spouse, this is the time you need each other. Communicating with my husband helped me to grieve our daughter's death, sometimes all you need is an ear to listen to what you're feeling and thinking with no judgment or even to validate that what you're feeling is normal - although there is no normal in grief.

Take care of yourself, only you know your limits.

-Whitney

Mother to Alexis Mae and Miranda Lee
http://stillmlg.blogspot.com/?m=1

*NOW IS THE TIME TO CARE FOR YOUR
BROKEN HEART AND DO WHAT WON'T
MAKE YOUR LOSS ANY HARDER.*

Walking along life's road after a miscarriage/stillbirth can be very difficult.

I've lost 5 heartbeats as early as 1995 with my last one on July 30, 2009. I'm here to let you know, there are no rules to grieving. Take your time, do what feels right to you and don't ever feel pressured to make excuses.

My path has been learning to live without a heartbeat. I've cried, screamed, laughed hysterically and lashed out at everyone around me. Learn to share your grief, yet know it's acceptable to hide under the covers of your bed all day. There is no time limit to grief, you will cherish your baby's memory for the rest of your life. Accept that your baby existed, your baby deserves to be acknowledged and do not let anyone tell you to stop 'dwelling on it.'

I've attended "In remembrance of" support groups, participated in "Bereavement Day" and joined online support groups. There are days when I won't get out of bed, cry all day and fall asleep as if to push away all the grief. Those are called my "Ostrich Days" because I bury my head in the sands of life. There are days when I can attend baby showers, gender reveal parties and such. Yet there are also stormy days when I miss those events and throw a pity party or cry in grief.

During my sunny days, I can hold a baby and be genuinely

happy for the mommy. I've helped organize baby showers and it felt right to do so. Please don't feel as if you're being "fake" if you force a smile when a baby wants to play peek-a-boo peering from Mom's shoulder. Everything you do, everything you feel and everything you say is acceptable.

Make sure your baby is remembered, say their name out loud and let others know it's fine to "talk about it." You do what you need to do, not what others say is acceptable. Your body, your baby, your broken heart and damn it, it's your life. Don't let anybody bully you, guilt you or make you feel ashamed. I've gone to the beach with a friend, turned on some music and danced while screaming our lungs out. We laughed, cried, screamed, danced, sang and howled at the moon. There was so much freedom and release that night. Some men tried to make a move on us and wouldn't take no for an answer. We finally pretended to be lovers and they ran away from us. We laughed so hard at the look on their faces.

So from one mama to another, you do YOU! There is no shame in what you do, none at all. Hide in your bed all day or get up and attend that baby shower, the decision is yours and yours alone.

I've been given a second chance at love with a man who became my husband on 11/11/11. I am also a stepmother to three handsome boys and a doggy mother to my baby girl,

Princess Abella Cordelia Van Etten. Yes, that is her name. I've become the greatest Auntie/Tia ever and loved my friends' babies as I would my own.

I'm grateful for my faith in God, my family, my pastor & church family and everyone who loves and supports me. I've recently been spoiling and loving my baby nephew, Kai Wade. He is now 9 months old and the love of this Tia's life. He has brought so much healing, love, peace and happiness with his mischevious, sparkling eyes and toothy smiles. Despite all of the heartache, pain, grief and sorrow, there is sunshine on cloudy days.

Namaste,

Sandra Lee Van Etten.

Josiah Daniel's Mommy

YOU DO WHAT YOU NEED TO DO, NOT WHAT OTHERS SAY IS ACCEPTABLE. YOUR BODY, YOUR BABY, YOUR BROKEN HEART AND DAMN IT, IT'S YOUR LIFE.

DEAR MAMA,

I see you. I see you holding onto your baby's tiny urn with tears streaming down your face. I see you sobbing in your dark room. I see you hunched over your photographs, trying to memorize every little detail of your child's beautiful face. I see you standing in the nursery, still trying to make sense of your child's absence. I see you struggling to get out of bed in the morning. I see you at the party trying to hide in the corner so you don't have to make small talk. I see you shaking your fists at God, begging Him to give your baby back. I see you fighting back the tears as you walk past the kid section at the store.

I see you.

I see you sitting in your car for an extra few minutes so you can finish listening to the song that reminds you of your child. I see you standing in the card section of the store, reading each and every one, searching for the perfect birthday card for him. I see you putting on your remembrance jewelry before you leave for work in the morning. I see you leaving toys your child would have loved by his headstone. I see you staring up at the sky in amazement as you discover the special message from above.

I see you.

I see your strength. I see your courage. I see your love.

I see your motherhood.

I see all of these things because I, too, am a bereaved mother. I wear the same worn out shoes that are needed for this treacherous journey. My heart aches, too. And my mind is also exhausted from all the unanswered questions. I have spent years replaying the final days of my daughter's life in my mind. Wondering what I could have done differently - what I would have done differently if I had known what was to come. I have carried guilt, regret, and anger. I blamed myself and felt like a failure. I wondered what I did to deserve this. The truth is, there is nothing that could have been done differently. No one deserves this. Not I and not you. We are not failures. **We are warriors.**

As hard as life after loss is, I have also learned many new and beautiful things. I now know how to love with my whole heart. I know what true love is and that it is never ends. You know these things, too. I know you will always love your child. You will always be hers, and she will always be yours. You are forever bound by that very special kind of love that only mother and child can share.

I see the fierceness in your eyes and the intensity in your heart. You are the strongest, bravest, and most beautiful mother there is. When the waves of grief are crashing down on you and you are worried you might actually drown this time, please remember one thing - you are not alone. We are here, and we will ride those waves with you. We will remember you child with you. It won't always be okay, but you can do this. You can get through today. Don't think about tomorrow. Just think about now. You can do this, mama. I believe in you.

I see you.

Love,

Lori

Elliot's Mama
https://walkingwithelliot.com/

WE ARE NOT FAILURES.
WE ARE WARRIORS.

CONTRIBUTORS' RESOURCES

WEBSITES AND BLOGS:

Emily R Long – Life Archaeologist: http://emilyrlong.com

Amie Lands – http://www.amielandsauthor.com

Amy Lied - https://doggiebagsnotdiaperbags.wordpress.com/

Anna Stanfield - http://www.letterstolillianblig.com

Bethany Stewart – EmbersandArrows

Bonnie Luttkus – http://www.lifewithyou1222.com

Christine Markowski - www.asareikimaster.wordpress.com

Danielle Ridgway - jensengrey.com

Darcie Champagne - www.lostlullabies.weebly.com

Diane DeLuzio - www.sgtstevendeluzio.com

Heather Kimble - www.hannahsheartandlove.org

Jolissa Skow - http://www.letterstojonah.com/ And http://www.courageousmothers.com

Kayla Bordon - Findinghannahrae.wordpress.com

Kristin Hernandez - www.sunlightindecember.com

Liz Mannegren - www.mommymannegren.com

Megan Baker - http://www.innerworldvillage.com.au/

Melissa Foley - www.wordpress.com/lachlanslove
Rachel Whalen - https://anunexpectedfamilyouting.wordpress.com/
Rebecca Harris - https://littlenutbrownhareblog.wordpress.com/
Till Heike-Woods - www.thestilllifeproject.org
Whitney Gealta - http://stillmlg.blogspot.com/?m=1
Lori Davis - https://walkingwithelliot.com

FACEBOOK PAGES:

Invisible Mothers: http://facebook.com/InvisibleMothers
Emma Eva: Our Journey with Trisomy 18: https://www.facebook.com/Emma-Eva-Our-Journey-with-Trisomy-18-535725723249338/
Emma's Footprints: https://www.facebook.com/EmmaKsfootprints
Christine Markowski: www.facebook.com/BellinghamReikiwithChristine
Danielle Ridgway: https://www.facebook.com/MyJensenGrey/
Darcie Champagne: https://www.facebook.com/lostlullabies/
Kayla Bordon: Grieve out loud
Megan Baker: Earth Mamas of Angel Babies - https://www.facebook.com/groups/1736383746607802/

Till Heike-Woods: Still Life Project

INSTAGRAM:

Emily Long - @long.emily
Amelia Kowalisyn - @KowalisynKiddos
Anna Stanfield - @letterstolillian
Danielle Ridgway @danii_ridgway

ADDITIONAL RESOURCES

Emily Long Books: www.emilyrlong.com/books
Still Standing Magazine: www.stillstandingmag.com
Still Mothers: www.stillmothers.com
A Bed for My Heart: www.abedformyheart.com
PALS (Pregnancy After Loss Support): www.
pregnancyafterlosssupport.com
On Coming Alive: www.oncomingalive.com
Grieving Parents Support Network: www.grievingparents.net

Made in the USA
Columbia, SC
07 June 2021

39376210R00134